UNAPOLOGETIC

On Purpose

UNAPOLOGETIC
On Purpose

THE INSIDE-OUT APPROACH TO IMPACTFUL LEADERSHIP

KIM KENNEY-ROCKWAL, MBA, SPHR

Publishing support provided by
Ignite Press
55 Shaw Ave. Suite 204
Clovis, CA 93612
www.IgnitePress.us

ISBN: 979-8-9953280-0-1
ISBN: 979-8-9953280-1-8 (Hardcover)
ISBN: 979-8-9953280-2-5 (E-book)

For bulk purchases and for booking, contact:

Kim Kenney-Rockwal
Kim@kimkenneyrockwal.com
kimkenneyrockwal.com

Library of Congress Control Number: 2026905076

Cover design by Lilik Hariawan
Edited by Zoe Herold
Interior design by Jetlaunch

FIRST EDITION

*This book is dedicated to my Nana and
my Dad who are now my angels.*

*Nana, thank you for being my first example of strength
wrapped in devotion. Your unwavering faith in me planted the
seeds of confidence long before I understood how deeply
I would need them. You showed me that kindness and
courage can coexist, and that true power
always begins within.*

*Dad, thank you for teaching me grit, sacrifice, and the value
of relationships and hard work, through countless life lessons
and conversations during our drives back and forth.
You celebrated my independence, nurtured my curiosity,
and challenged me to lead, stand tall, use my voice, and keep
going when the road felt uncertain. Your belief in my ability to
figure things out gave me permission to trust myself, and
that has shaped every chapter of my life. You are, and
always will be, my true star!*

*Your love, lessons, and legacy live in every word of this book.
I carry you with me, always.*

Acknowledgments

Writing this book has been one of the most humbling and meaningful experiences of my life, shaped by endless conversations, acts of generosity, and countless situational lessons.

No meaningful work is ever done alone.

To my family: Scott, your unwavering love and support made this journey possible, and you remind me daily that I never walk alone. Emily and Ryan, you are my inspiration. Watching you grow into independent, curious, and resilient adults is my greatest joy, and you challenge me to lead with integrity, heart, and purpose.

To my review board, Cindy, Dawn, Joanne, Kerry, Pauline, and Suzanne; thank you for your encouragement, candor, and thoughtful edits. Your support made this book stronger.

And to the leaders, women, and change-makers reading this: you are the reason this book exists. May these pages remind you to trust your voice, honor your truth, and lead unapologetically—on purpose.

This book is for you.

Table of Contents

Prologue: My WHY

This book is for you.

Especially for women.
Especially for those early in their careers, wrestling with ambition and doubt at the same time.
Especially for anyone who has never had a coach in their corner before.

> **Women, far too often, struggle more with self-worth, confidence, and granting themselves permission to lead.**

The goal is simple: to give you access. Not only to tools and strategies, but to the "why" behind them. To illuminate the patterns that hold people back, including the tough ones while offering practical ways to build focus, courage, and confidence.

Across countless roles, industries, and leadership levels, one truth has stood out: development is not equal. The disparity of women being held back from their full potential cannot continue. Women, far too often, struggle more with self-worth, confidence, and granting themselves permission to lead.

That disparity cannot continue. This book won't solve the disparity by itself, but it can help close the gap—one reflection, one insight, one story, one act of bravery at a time.

And if you're holding this book, something important is already true about you:

You are open.
You are curious.
You are more ready than you think.

This book was born from equal parts passion, purpose, and conviction.

Over the years, it has been impossible not to notice a trend in the professional world: polished books and shiny titles offered by people with minimal real-world leadership experience, yet presented as universal truth. Rather than stay frustrated, I have redirected that energy into something far more meaningful: sharing hard-earned lessons from more than three decades in Human Resources, coaching, and leadership development.

Those decades have been spent in the trenches with executive leaders, new managers, full teams, and individuals navigating the real, messy, and often exhilarating work of growth. Many of my clients who experienced that development were selected by their organizations—chosen, nudged, or flagged for coaching.

But what about everyone else?

What about:

- The individual contributors who want more but don't know how to get there.

- The rising stars who haven't yet been given access to coaching.
- The first-time managers who are determined to lead well but are unsure where to start.

In the opening chapters, you'll find personal stories. We all carry formative childhood moments that shape the leader you become. Reflecting on your own is where your coaching journey begins. From there, the book moves into everyday workplace challenges that influence your leadership style. You'll see both wins and missteps, paired with reflections and prompts to help you build your own wisdom, not just absorb someone else's.

Additional coaching reflections, activities, and leadership prompts not included in the book can be accessed here: https://www.unapologeticonpurpose.com

Later chapters explore the transition from peer to boss, overcoming fear, managing up, and micro-lessons from coaching clients, followed by a career action plan to help you chart your next bold move.

And throughout the journey, the invitation is this:

- Take bold risks—even when fear whispers "not yet."
- Pursue the career path that actually excites you.
- Say yes to stretch opportunities that grow your skillset.
- Make small, meaningful choices that strengthen your confidence.
- Lift other women as you rise.
- **Thrive—in whatever you choose to pursue.**

Progress doesn't always look dramatic. Sometimes the bravest leap is a tiny step forward.

As the saying reminds us: **"By the yard, it's hard. By the inch, it's a cinch."**

Go at your own pace. Keep moving. Build momentum. The only requirement is to begin.

After years of conversations about growth, leadership, and development, it is a privilege to finally place these lessons and stories in your hands.

Lets go!

1

"Great" Inspiration

Role Models Come from Many Places

Isn't it strange how the smallest discoveries often become the most meaningful?

As I sorted through a box of old cards one quiet afternoon, searching for the perfect Mother's Day message, I found something far more powerful than a printed sentiment. Tucked away among forgotten envelopes was a handwritten note from over 25 years ago—a simple, heartfelt thank-you from my grandmother, Nana, for stopping by with Mother's Day gifts. That one piece of paper, scrawled in her familiar handwriting, stirred something deep within me. In that moment, I was reminded that true inspiration often finds us when we're not looking.

Nana—known affectionately as "Great" by my toddler children at the time—was more than just a grandmother. She was my anchor, my compass, and the fiercest woman I've ever known. Her real name was Gladys, but to me, she embodied something greater than any title. Raised during the Great Depression, she carried the scars and strength of that time into every corner of her life. She taught me, by example, that tenacity is a form of love, and that speaking up is sometimes the kindest thing you can do.

She never sat me down to deliver life lessons. She lived them. Every day. And I watched. I watched as she navigated life with dignity, wit, and a no-nonsense attitude that somehow never sacrificed kindness. She had a rare combination of sharp edges and open arms.

One of my most vivid memories with her came when I was 12 years old. We were at a picnic on a blazing hot summer day, waiting in an agonizingly long line for food. After nearly an hour in the sun, a woman with her large family slipped into line ahead of us. Without hesitation, Nana stepped forward and addressed the woman directly. There was no hesitation, no apology, just a firm insistence that fairness mattered. She didn't yell. She didn't belittle. She simply corrected. And the woman, to everyone's surprise, stepped back in line. That was Nana. You didn't get away with injustice, not on her watch.

This sense of justice wasn't just personal; it was professional. Nana worked as a police matron, where being tough and fair wasn't optional—it was survival. She had no tolerance for dishonesty or excuses and yet remained deeply compassionate. She believed in everyone's ability to do better and held them to it.

Even in her 70s, she laced up roller skates to join us grandchildren at the rink, proving that age was no excuse for sitting life out. And into her 80s, she remained a force to be reckoned with. I remember taking her to the bank one Saturday morning. When she didn't return after 20 minutes, I went inside. A teller directed me to the manager's office. Apparently, someone had cut in front of her in line and Nana wasn't letting it slide. What started as a quiet confrontation ended in a heated conversation with the bank manager. I didn't even need to ask what happened. I already knew someone had broken the rules, and Nana had made sure they knew it.

What struck me most was that she never fought for herself alone, she fought for what was right. She modeled a version of strength that had nothing to do with dominance and everything to do with integrity. She didn't argue to win; she stood up to remind others—and herself—that fairness and respect are non-negotiable.

Leaning into discomfort often leads to clarity, to truth, to change.

Later in life, during executive coaching, my coach once asked me, "Kim, where did your love of conflict come from?" At first, I laughed. But deep down, I knew. It came from Nana. Not because she loved conflict—but because she never ran from it. She faced it head-on when the situation called for courage. She showed me that leaning into discomfort often leads to clarity, to truth, to change.

Her legacy lives on in the way I approach challenges, in my unwillingness to be passive in the face of wrong, and in my insistence that values are only real if we're willing to defend them.

We all draw inspiration from different people at different stages of our lives—family, teachers, coaches, clergy, friends. Some come into our lives like lightning; others are a slow, steady flame. For me, "Great" was both. She was my lightning and my fire.

So, as you reflect on your own life, ask yourself:

Who shaped your voice? Your courage? Your conviction?

Who stood behind you—or even better, beside you—when you needed it most?

Because if you look closely, you'll likely find that your greatest inspiration wasn't someone who gave you answers, but someone who showed you how to ask the right questions and never back down from living your truth.

2

The Bus Maneuver

The Right Bus

Where do you draw your strength from?

It's a question that invites reflection, one that has resurfaced many times over the years. Strength rarely comes from perfection or predictability. More often, it's forged through disruption, hardship, and the quiet resilience that forms when someone is both supported and left to figure things out alone.

A family divided by divorce when only five years old could have meant chaos, but a small circle of consistent, caring people created a foundation that I'll never forget. Their steadiness became my lifeline. Yet it's just as true that many grow up without mirrors, without people who look like them, live like them, or understand where they come from. That kind of isolation can shape a person deeply. And sometimes, the greatest lessons come not from similarity, but from difference. They simply arrive in unfamiliar packaging.

At six, everything familiar disappeared—home, community, routines, safety. A move nearly eighty miles away landed my family in public housing, where the walls were thin, the sidewalks cracked, and the social rules could be summarized in two words: survive or become a target.

By ten, real-world education was happening on the sidewalks, stairwells, and bus stops of the neighborhood. Speaking up became a calculated risk. Disappearing became a skill. "Bob and weave" weren't metaphors; it was a strategy. Getting home after school required speed, situational awareness, and the ability to read a room—or a crowd—faster than most adults ever need to.

Every afternoon brought the same choice between two bus stops: 8 and 8A. One was closer to the apartment building, but if the bullies boarded that one, it wasn't an option. From a distance, a quick scan became routine—eyes alert, heartbeat quick. If the troublemakers loaded Bus 8, waiting for 8A was the only solution. If they crowded onto 8A, the long walk was the safer bet.

Neither path was truly safe. One led through woods and up a steep hill past ten buildings. The other meant sprinting past dark corners and alleyways where fists, insults, and intimidation waited. Every step home was strategic. Every day was an uninvited test of courage.

This wasn't ordinary childhood conflict, it was the slow erosion of safety. And yet, something powerful grew from it. Awareness. Grit. Intuition. The hard-won understanding of what it feels like to be invisible, and the even more important understanding of what it means to choose yourself anyway.

Eventually, circumstances shifted. The older bullies moved on to new schools and new routines. Along the way, a few trusted friends emerged, just enough to form a protective circle. A small band of kids who walked each other home, watched each other's backs, and refused to let fear win without a fight.

Safety didn't magically appear, but strength did. Friendship did. Courage did.

And the lesson has never stopped applying. Every one of us still faces a version of that bus stop.

In boardrooms, classrooms, workplaces, and conversations we're constantly assessing who holds power, who might harm us, and how to protect ourselves while still moving forward.

Consider this:

Who were *your* bullies—past or present?
What did they teach you, intentionally or not?
And what unexpected strength did you discover in yourself because of them?

Strength isn't always loud. Sometimes, it looks like waiting for the right bus. Sometimes, it's knowing when to walk away. And sometimes, it's as simple—and as profound—as walking a friend home.

3

Self-Reliance from the Village

How Distant Love Built Inner Strength

BLENDING TWO FAMILIES is never simple. When differences in parenting styles, money philosophies, and core values collide under one roof, chaos often follows. In this case, it became a perfect storm; two older stepbrothers raised without boundaries and younger stepsiblings shaped by the structure of a law-enforcement household. The combination didn't mesh. Ever curious and observant, a young "Nancy Drew" version of myself emerged, constantly investigating household dynamics and catching mischief red-handed.

My stepfather at the center of it all was a man seemingly stuck in adolescence. Ambition held little interest for him; professionally, the bar remained low, yet an inflated sense of self-worth persisted. Routine ruled his world. Every Friday night, like clockwork, he planted himself at the kitchen table with a drink in hand. Hours passed, bottles emptied, and the weekly ritual unfolded—slurred words, lost balance, then an unsteady path to bed.

My bedroom sat directly above the kitchen. Whenever voices rose in anger, my quiet footsteps made their way downstairs, pretending to rummage through the refrigerator—an early emotional temperature check. If his anger turned toward my brother or mother, stepping in became non-negotiable. That cycle repeated itself far too often.

And yet, even in the darkest moments, there was a lifeline: a village 80 miles away, but always within reach. That village, comprised of my Dad and Nana, offered something chaos could never steal, my hope, resilience, and a blueprint for self-reliance.

During one of the most violent moments in our household, I called my village. I stood outwardly steady, speaking with confidence and resolve, even as fear shook me beneath the surface. I held my ground, waiting, listening, anchoring myself to the sound of safe voices.

Within 90 minutes, they arrived, without hesitation and without questions. They pulled my brother out and made sure the cycle would never continue. Knowing he would be safe, I chose to stay behind, protecting my mother when she was most vulnerable.

By choosing responsibility over retreat, I discovered something lasting: I could stand on my own. That moment forged my self-reliance and taught me to trust myself when the stakes were highest.

Self-reliance does not mean standing alone. It means knowing exactly when to reach for the hands that will hold you up. It means recognizing that your voice matters, even when it trembles. It means understanding that survival can be a collective effort, and strength can be found in the embrace of those who remind you of your worth.

That village shows up every day: in values, in confidence, in courage. They are the reason for a steady spine, a clear voice, and an unwavering belief that dysfunction is not destiny.

The village may not always be nearby. But their belief in you can echo through the hardest nights and fuel you through the brightest days.

Ask yourself:

Who is part of *your* village?
Who reminds *you* of your strength when the world feels heavy?
And how might you build self-reliance—not in spite of the noise, but because of it?

4

The 24-Hour Gut

Trusting Your Inner Compass

Do you ever feel that immediate signal in your gut to act or avoid? And are you listening? On my first day in a new management role, crisp fall air carried that familiar sense of beginning again. After working all day, briefly meeting the management team and both shifts of employees, I started getting ready to call it a day. Two parking exits stood ahead: one for administration and one for production staff. I started toward the administration exit, ready to drive home. Then something stopped me.

A car packed with second-shift employees rolled past, releasing a thick cloud of smoke. My mind jumped straight into risk assessment: *What were they doing on break? What could this mean for safety?* The possibilities weren't positive. That's when my gut reacted; fast, clear, undeniable. **Follow that car.**

I listened.

Uncertain where it would lead and unsure what to expect, my quiet pursuit continued until the vehicle stopped in the parking lot of a fast-food restaurant. No one headed inside for food. Instead, they pulled out a bong and began passing it around... in plain sight. My stomach dropped. They were preparing to return to work under the influence.

I have no company contacts yet. No phone numbers. Not even an organizational chart. All I had was intuition and the certainty that ignoring what I saw wasn't an option.

That night, I wrestled with the decision. Speak up and risk appearing naïve on day one? Or say nothing and allow the behavior to continue unchecked?

The next morning, I went to the President and reported what I saw. He laughed and said, "You've been here less than 24 hours. Who are you to say we have a drug problem?"

Shrinking would have been easy. Silence would have been simpler. But neither happened. For the rest of the week, I raised the issue again and again. I kept the pressure on by asking questions. By Friday, the tone shifted. The President agreed to bring in an undercover officer from the security firm. For the next month, daily intel rolled in about second-shift activities.

What was uncovered was worse than imagined. Working with local law enforcement, we coordinated a sting operation. This led to multiple arrests and terminations related to narcotics use, sale, and distribution on company property.

There was no parade. No recognition. No moment of celebration for the intuition and persistence that sparked the investigation.

But the truth was known and that was enough.

Unfortunately, it also revealed the deeper dysfunction rampant through this workplace. I learned the price of the truth quickly, but trust in leadership dissolved just as fast.

One afternoon, during a particularly tense executive meeting, the CEO removed his shoe and hurled it at the CFO—inside a glass-walled conference room, visible to staff. That moment snapped everything into focus. I went to the restroom and stared into the mirror and saw the truth clearly: *This place isn't right.* The job I thought would be a step forward in my career had exposed a culture of chaos, ego, and unchecked power. Still, I walked back into that meeting room-steady, composed, stronger than I felt and met the conflict head-on.

That's the thing about trusting your gut, it rarely feels comfortable. It rarely earns applause. But it always pulls you toward something more honest.

The dysfunction only escalated. Each day felt like an episode of workplace reality TV: temper tantrums, public shaming, unethical choices. Yet the President's offer of high salaries kept people locked in place. Golden handcuffs clinked loudly in every hallway leaving employees trapped.

I made the choice to leave.

That year was grueling and pushed every limit. Hard conversations became routine. I was in over my head, treading water at the deep end of the pool without a life jacket. The answers weren't always clear, but my curiosity remained constant. I read every white paper I could find, studied them, absorbed them, and tested them in real time. I practiced confidence before I believed it. Then one day, practice transformed into truth.

That's the thing about trusting your gut, it rarely feels comfortable. It rarely earns applause. But it always pulls you toward something more honest.

Consider this:

When was the last time your inner voice spoke louder than your fear?
What might shift if courage outweighed comfort, even when the room disagreed?
And what lessons become available not *despite* the hard places—but *because* of them?

Sometimes the greatest growth doesn't come from finding the right place… but from realizing with absolute clarity that you're not in it and choosing to move.

5

From "Can't" to Can!

Rewriting the Story in Your Head

FROM THE EARLIEST moments in life, we're often conditioned to focus on what is wrong instead of what is possible. Don't believe me?

Let me take you back to my daughter Emily's kindergarten year. I couldn't wait for our first parent-teacher conference. Emily spent every spare moment playing "school," always as the teacher, never the student. It was clear, even then, that she was a natural leader, curious and confident, the kind of child any educator would be thrilled to have in their class.

So I arrived, ready to hear glowing praise. But instead, the teacher began with, "There's a problem."

My heart sank.

"What's wrong?" I asked.

The teacher leaned in and said with a serious tone: "Emily colors outside the lines."

I blinked.

That was the *problem*? My immediate reaction was joy: "That's wonderful! I want my daughter to challenge boundaries, to see the world creatively, to explore beyond the edges."

But the teacher replied firmly, "In kindergarten, we color in the lines."

And just like that, I saw how early the messaging begins. Stay within limits. Follow the rules. Don't rock the boat.

This moment stayed with me and I began to connect the dots. In the workplace, I've seen this same pattern play out again and again. Talented individuals, full of potential, hold themselves back when asked to stretch. When challenged to grow, many instinctively retreat. Not because they can't do it, but because somewhere along the way, they were taught to believe they couldn't.

Let me tell you about Vicky.

Vicky was a rockstar Executive Assistant; hyper-organized, fiercely protective of her leader's time, and excellent at juggling priorities. Her work ethic was unmatched, which is why her leader wanted her to go on a high-visibility acquisition project. A stretch assignment. A big deal.

But as soon as she was assigned, everything shifted. Vicky became quiet. Distant. She avoided eye contact and peppered conversations with self-deprecating remarks.

We sat down, and after peeling back the layers, her resistance wasn't about the task. It went deep back to a moment in childhood that left a scar she still carried at age 55.

At just ten years old, Vicky had been preparing for her flute solo at a school concert. She was nervous but excited. Just before stepping on stage, her father told her he had to leave. When she asked why, he said work was more important. And besides, she wasn't going to be a professional musician anyway.

To a child, that wasn't just disappointing, it was a message. *You're not good enough. You're not worth the time.*

That belief took root. For decades, every time Vicky faced something new or challenging, those words echoed back. Even when the assignment came from a place of trust and recognition, her inner dialogue—those old emotional tapes—told her she was destined to fail.

But here's the good news: YOU can change the tape.

Together, we broke down her project into smaller, manageable pieces. We celebrated the wins; every step forward, every bit of progress. It was important for Vicky to see herself through my eyes filled with potential and not the mirror that had been disappointing her for so long. Slowly, she began to rewrite her internal script. Each win chipped away at the old story. She started saying, "I can" more than "I can't."

This wasn't just a transformation in task execution, it was a shift in belief. A breakthrough.

Here's the question for you:

What outdated beliefs or internal tapes are holding you back?
What stories are you still telling yourself that limit your potential?

Because your potential isn't defined by the lines others draw for you, it's defined by how boldly you're willing to color outside them.

This isn't just a challenge for individual contributors like Vicky. I've seen this self-doubt echo through boardrooms and executive suites. No one is immune.

Stop fixating on what you *can't* do.
Start focusing on what you **CAN** do.

Because your potential isn't defined by the lines others draw for you, it's defined by how boldly you're willing to color outside them.

6

Don't Touch the Cake!

Elevate Your Brand – Don't Reinforce Misperceptions

IF YOU'VE EVER worked long-term in an organization, you know how difficult it can be to shake off outdated perceptions, especially those formed early in your career. When you first step into a role, you might not have all the polish, experience, or professional savvy you'll develop later. Yet some managers never update the lens through which they view you. Even as you grow, evolve, and excel, they may still see the younger, less refined version of you. And that outdated perception can quietly stall your advancement.

That's exactly what happened to Becky.

Fresh out of college, Becky started as an analyst. Bright and hardworking, she was quick to learn and eager to contribute. But like many early-career professionals, she occasionally stumbled; speaking out of turn or making political missteps. Over time, Becky built a stellar reputation for her deep knowledge of the company and its products. She rotated through several departments, mastered her roles, and became a go-to expert.

Yet every time she applied for a manager position, she was passed over. Again, and again.

She started to feel what I call "POPO"—**Passed Over, Pissed Off**.

Despite her excellence in individual contributor roles, she wasn't being seen as leadership material. Why? Because the perception of "young Becky" still lingered.

We worked together to shift that narrative.

Becky began refining her communication; more measured, more strategic, more executive. She took on high-visibility projects and positioned herself to present key updates directly to senior leaders. She also thought carefully about her presence, how she dressed, how she showed up in meetings, how she wrote emails. She wasn't just doing great work; she was **being seen** doing great work.

And then… it happened. Becky was promoted to manager.

Six months in, she was thriving. Her team loved working with her, and she delivered strong results. She was finally being recognized as the leader she had become.

Then came a moment I'll never forget.

It was a celebration for a senior executive's milestone birthday. Executives, managers, and staff were gathered to sing "Happy Birthday." As the cake was rolled out, Becky started walking toward it. I instinctively grabbed her arm and whispered, *"Don't touch the cake."*

Confused, she whispered back, *"I'm just going to help cut and help pass it out."*

I tightened my grip. This time, a bit firmer: *"DON'T. TOUCH. THE. CAKE."*
She rolled her eyes, but I smiled, "We'll talk after."

Here's the thing, Becky was no longer the eager helper in the room. She was now a manager. A leader. And even though her intention was good, stepping in to cut the cake would have reinforced an old image of her; one she had worked so hard to outgrow.

Sometimes, without realizing it, we **undo our own progress**. A small act—helping, serving, fetching coffee—can feel polite or harmless. But if it fits a stereotype or an old perception others have of you, doing it repeatedly can signal: *"This is still who I am."*

I've made this mistake, too. Early in my executive journey, I once offered to get coffee for my team during a meeting; just being polite. No big deal, right?

Wrong.

From then on, I became "the coffee person." My male peers—also executives—expected it. I had unintentionally reinforced a stereotype and diminished my standing at the table. I corrected it quickly, but the lesson stuck.

Be helpful—but be **strategic**.
Be kind—but be **aware**.
Be supportive—but never at the cost of your **leadership image**.

This happens to women far too often. We are conditioned to nurture, accommodate, and make ourselves smaller for the comfort of others. We soften our competence with self-deprecation, mistaking humility for safety. But leadership demands something different. At work, when you are building or reinventing your brand, it's essential to manage how others perceive you. You must be intentional about how you show up. Own your strengths and be clear about your value.

So, when you find yourself at the metaphorical cake table... pause.

You've worked too hard to be seen differently.
Don't touch the cake.

Core Lesson

Even as you evolve, others may still see the "old you." It's not enough to do great work, you have to *strategically* show that you've grown. Every interaction, behavior, and choice either reinforces an outdated brand or strengthens your current, elevated one.

Summary: You have worked hard to grow into the professional you are today. Don't let old perceptions define your future. Every choice is a chance to reinforce your brand as the capable, strategic leader you've become. When you find yourself at the "cake table" moment... pause. You don't have to prove your value by serving. You prove it by leading. Take some time to work on these reflection questions and potential stretch assignments in this area.

Reflection Activity: Think about how you are currently perceived at work.

- Are there outdated impressions others may still hold about you?
- Have you unintentionally reinforced them by doing things out of habit, helpfulness, or comfort?
- How often do you rely on self-deprecating humor, and what is it costing you?

Now, ask yourself: *What do I want to be known for today and what needs to change so others can see that version of me?*

To grow as a leader, you must actively manage how others perceive you and stop unconsciously reinforcing outdated or limiting images of who you used to be.

Supporting Insights

1. **Perception drives opportunity.**
   Talent and results matter, but advancement often depends on how others *see* you. If you're still viewed through an old lens, your growth can go unnoticed.
2. **Small actions send big signals.**
   Simple gestures—like cutting a cake or volunteering for small tasks—can unintentionally reinforce outdated roles or stereotypes, especially for women in leadership.
3. **Intent vs. Impact matters.**
   You can have the best intentions (to help, support, or serve), but the *impact* might subtly undermine your authority or leadership presence.
4. **Rebranding takes conscious effort.**
   Like Becky, you must refine your presence, communication, and visibility to reflect who you are now, not who you were years ago.
5. **Strategic leadership is about discernment.**
   True leadership requires knowing when to step forward… and when to step back. Sometimes, restraint is the most powerful move you can make.

7

Unapologetically Confident in Pink

Leading with Grit, Grace, and a Pop of Color

Working as a woman executive in a male-dominated industry is challenging enough. Add a culture built around late-night drinking and locker-room banter, and suddenly the environment tests not just someone's competence but their confidence.

That was my reality.

Earning a seat at the executive table took years of grit and dedication. Becoming a Vice President before I was 40 was a milestone worth celebrating, but once there, it became clear that the real challenge wasn't earning the title. The real challenge was keeping ground in a room where a woman's confidence was mistaken for arrogance, where professionalism was defined by outdated norms, and where authority wasn't given... it had to be claimed.

Every day required resolve. Noise, ego, and resistance had to be pushed through just to do the work and advocate for the people being served. The goal was to redefine what leadership looked like; to bring strategy, empathy, and credibility to human resources at the highest level. But change that disrupts the status quo never happens quietly.

One spring afternoon, after a full day of work, Nick—a manufacturing leader—smirked, "Oh, half day today?" It was his backhanded way of signaling that he planned to stay all day and night. His lack of a life outside of work wasn't a badge of honor, and it certainly wasn't something he had the right to impose on anyone else. I ignored the comment. Moments later, he threw another jab, "You know, you'd be more successful if you wore less pink."

Change that disrupts the status quo never happens quietly.

I smiled as wide as I could, showing both dimples and shouted confidently back, "I've got a news flash for you, I'm already successful."

The comment lingered, not because self-doubt set in, but because the intent behind it became clear. Nick wasn't criticizing a color; he wanted to make me question who I am and the title I had. Pink stood out. It broke his mold of what power should look like. He wanted smaller, quieter, less visible.

I heard a familiar voice, a father's reminder: *"Never let those people rent space in your head."*

The next morning, in the brightest pink suit, matching shoes, and my unapologetically pink lipstick showed up to work. If I could have dyed my hair pink that morning, I probably would have. I confidently walked straight to Nick's office and opened with, "News flash: pink will be worn whenever I want."

And I did… every day that week.

Over time, the message behind his comment became unmistakable: it was never about color. It was about control. It was an attempt to chip away at my confidence, to shrink my influence, to reinforce outdated power structures in a space where meaningful impact was already happening.

But true leadership isn't about blending in. It's about standing tall, especially when standing out.

Takeaways:

- **Don't apologize for being visible.** Visibility isn't vanity, it's leadership. When you stand out, you give others permission to do the same.
- **Challenge outdated norms.** Progress happens when we refuse to conform to comfort zones that no longer serve us.
- **Protect your confidence.** Don't let anyone's opinion become your limitation. Your confidence is your credibility.
- **Redefine professionalism.** Authenticity, not assimilation, drives trust and results.

8

Know When It's Time to Go

Embrace the Inner Tug-of-War

THERE ARE MOMENTS in your career that feel like destiny. For me, that moment was finding a company that truly aligned with my **core values** and a mission I wholeheartedly believed in. I considered myself incredibly fortunate. Every day, I had the opportunity to help develop the next generation of leaders in the very community I called home. The work was meaningful, the team was strong, and the program was thriving.

We were building something special.

Processes were improving, our reputation was growing, and the message from the outside was clear: *This program is hard, but excellent.* My team and I took pride in that. We had built a high-performing, purpose-driven unit. It was the kind of momentum every leader hopes for.

And then, without warning, it was all taken away.

Leadership decided to pull my team and create a brand-new department. That kind of organizational change didn't surprise me, I was used to the corporate world. What **surprised** me was how I found out: **not from my boss, but from my team.**

My direct reports received vague calendar invites to meet with the VP. Naturally, they came to me to ask what was going on. The problem? I had no idea either.

We were supposed to be a leadership company—teaching best practices, emotional intelligence, and strategic communication—and yet, behind the scenes, leadership was doing the opposite. No transparency. No inclusion. No respect.

When change happens, people crave communication. They don't expect all the answers, but they do expect **honesty**, **clarity**, and **dignity**. In the absence of communication, people create their own stories. And those stories are almost always rooted in **fear**.

Was it a performance issue?
Was someone getting fired?
Were we being evaluated behind closed doors?

It didn't take long for rumors to spread, and with them, productivity and trust began to crumble.

Eventually, my team was reassigned. No plan to backfill. No support. No acknowledgment of the impact. For over a year, I held the weight; managing what had once been a multi-person job, navigating a pandemic, and doing everything I could to keep the program's standards high. I gave everything I had, over and over again.

And when I finally handed in my resignation—a long, thoughtful letter detailing every step of the decline—I was met with surprise.

Surprise?

I had asked for help.
I had raised red flags.
I had stayed longer than I should have.

I knew then that I had been in a silent tug-of-war. My head knew something was wrong. My heart still believed in the mission. But over time, my values, the very reason I joined, were no longer reflected in the company's actions.

And that was the line.
That was the moment I knew: *It's time to go.*

The hardest part wasn't leaving.
It was **admitting** that the place I once loved no longer aligned with who I was.

Ask Yourself This Powerful Question: "If nothing changes in the next 6 months, would I still want to be here?"

If the answer is no, no need to tug anymore. Let go of the rope.

Reflection Activity:

- Are you ignoring your internal tug-of-war?
- What values brought you to your current role and are they still being honored?
- What has your inner voice been telling you lately?

9

What Can You Learn from a Broom Closet?

Redefining Power, Presence, and Purpose

I'VE TOLD THIS story countless times because it reminds people of something simple, yet powerful: **stay true to your purpose, trust your instincts, and never let anyone bully you out of your values.**

I have just been assigned a new office. Not just any office, one located on "Executive Row." A pristine corridor lined with polished mahogany desks and leadership titles displayed like trophies. For some, this would have been a milestone. For me? It was a red flag.

I had spent months building trust in a culturally diverse, complex organization where Human Resources had long been viewed with skepticism. Slowly, we were turning the tide; creating a space of mutual respect, cultural understanding, and human connection. But moving to Executive Row? That was like putting a barrier between me and the very people I was there to support.

It would've sent the wrong message.
It would've said: "I'm one of them. You're on your own."
And I couldn't let that happen.

Leadership isn't about where you sit.
It's about how you show up.

So, I made the choice and proposed something radical: *Give me the broom closet.*

Yes, a literal broom closet, just off the cafeteria, cluttered with mops, vacuums, and utility supplies. It wasn't polished. It wasn't prestigious. But it was **awesome**.

My peers—mostly male leaders—rolled their eyes. Some mocked me. Others thought I was making a power play in reverse. But I didn't care. Because to me, leadership isn't about where you sit. It's about how you show up.

Making Space for Trust

At first, employees whispered when they passed by. They weren't sure what to make of it. But as days went on, they saw I wasn't there to spy… I was there to **listen**. To **understand**. To **support**.

Soon, I was invited to breakroom conversations and coffee chats. I learned about weekend plans, workplace frustrations, cultural misunderstandings, and personal celebrations. The broom closet gave me the clearest window into the **heartbeat of the organization**.

It became a place where employees could come with questions, concerns, and stories. A place where their voices were heard, without judgment or hierarchy. And because I was in their space, not behind an imposing desk, they began to trust. Not just me, but the entire concept of Human Resources as an advocate, not an adversary.

Leadership Without a Pedestal

The most remarkable thing? The deeper our relationships grew, the stronger the organization became. Employees shared gifts from their home countries: embroidered art from Vietnam, beautiful kimonos, small treasures from overseas trips. And one day, they organized a potluck, a celebration of unity and thanks. Every dish told a story. Every conversation bridged a gap. It felt like a gathering of the United Nations. And I knew: *this is what leadership looks like.*

It wasn't about power or prestige, just presence. It was a genuine human connection.

The Lesson of the Broom Closet

That small, cluttered room taught me more than any boardroom ever could.

It taught me that **titles are free**, but *respect is earned.*
It reminded me that **proximity builds trust**.
And most of all, it affirmed that **doing the right thing is often inconvenient, but always worth it.**

I tell this story to my graduate students and coaching clients because it holds one essential question:

What's your broom closet?
What principle are you willing to defend, even at a professional cost?
Where can you take a stand that puts *people before optics*?

The world doesn't need more leaders with perfect offices and polished resumes.
It needs more leaders who are willing to **get a little uncomfortable** to do what's right.

Reflection Activity:

- What illusion of power or prestige might be separating you from the people you serve?
- What does authentic leadership look like in your environment and are you modeling it?

10

Rising Together

Choosing Collaboration in a World That Teaches Competition

"When one woman rises, we all rise.
Let's stop competing for space and start creating it."
—Kim Kenney-Rockwal

WHY IS IT that some women still view other successful women as threats, rather than allies? It's a question I've asked myself many times over the course of my career. At nearly every stage, I've felt the sting of being seen not as a partner, but as competition—especially by other women in positions of leadership.

It wasn't because I was trying to take anyone's job. I was simply curious. I asked questions. I wanted to understand how leaders found success, what they would do differently, and how I could grow in my own journey. I wasn't trying to climb over anyone; I was trying to learn, to connect, to contribute.

But in environments where resources or opportunities feel limited, curiosity can be mistaken for ambition, and ambition may be seen as a threat.

Even when I hadn't yet had many female mentors or role models, I made a promise to myself: *If I ever rise, I'll reach back and pull others up too.*

That promise has shaped the leader I've become.

The Missed Opportunity

Not long ago, my team was navigating a complex, high-stakes project that required cross-functional collaboration. A woman in a key leadership position—who had every opportunity to empower, guide, and uplift—chose another path. She wielded her expertise like a weapon, asserting dominance instead of offering support.

Rather than using her knowledge to promote understanding, she used it to divide. Tina was exceptionally skilled at navigating organizational politics. She knew how to secure scarce resources, cascade communication effectively and gain buy-in from nearly anyone. But she also needed to be the smartest person in the room. Success had to point back to her leadership and her team. While she publicly endorsed collaboration, her actions told a different story. She withheld critical information, dismissed contributions that didn't originate from her team, and used judgment as a means of control by signaling who has permission to contribute and who does not. Influence, for her, came through manipulation rather than partnership.

Quietly, mistrust spread. Doubt took root and misperceptions about our department were planted and allowed to grow. Information was no longer a tool for progress, it became a power to be hoarded, not shared. What she missed was the greater opportunity. She could have been more than just a big title. **She could have been a mentor, a connector, a bridge between teams, especially for the non-management employees who looked up to her. Instead, she built walls.**

And while her actions slowed the work project down, the deeper damage lingered. Collaboration fractured and trust eroded. This had the possibility of strengthening leadership across the organization but became a lesson in what happens when power is chosen over purpose.

A Better Way Forward

This is not just a cautionary tale. It's a call to action.

Every woman in leadership has a choice: to compete or to collaborate, to tear down or to build up. When we choose collaboration, we create spaces where ideas flourish, teams thrive, and real innovation happens.

Collaboration is not about losing ground. It's about gaining momentum—together.

You don't lose anything by helping someone else succeed. In fact, when you lead with generosity and courage, your influence expands. Your legacy deepens.

Let's stop playing small by fighting over limited seats at the table. Let's build longer tables.

Reflection Prompt

- Have you ever been perceived as competitive when you were just trying to contribute?
- How did it make you feel and what did you learn from it?
- How do *you* respond when you see another woman rising?

11

You Have to Give to Get

Leaving a Legacy Behind

AT THE END of your career, what legacy do you want to leave behind?

If you're just beginning your professional journey, it isn't too early to ask that question. And if you're nearing the close of your career, it's worth reflecting on what people will truly remember about you.

The thing is, it won't be the last project you completed, the deadline you met, or the exhausting hoop jumping effort it took to coordinate a multi-level meeting. Those details fade. What endures is how you made people feel, especially in their uncomfortable moments. When they felt invisible, questioned whether they belonged, or were too afraid to speak up.

Giving of yourself is not a sacrifice, it is an intentional investment in people.

That investment doesn't require formal mentoring programs or scheduled check-ins. Sometimes it's as simple as noticing someone who is struggling and choosing to ask, *Are you okay?* Over time, trust, loyalty, and credibility are built one conversation at a time. This is the kind of legacy that outlives your title and your tenure.

Legacy leadership cannot be transactional. You don't invest in people expecting something in return. When you do, you miss the point entirely.

That was Tim's blind spot.

Tim was an experienced healthcare operations leader who had worked in organizations ranging from small practices to large, complex systems. He was charismatic and well-liked. On the surface, he appeared successful. However, to his many direct reports, Tim was a busy leader but not an impactful one.

His definition of success was rooted in transactions: metrics, productivity, turnover, and output. These elements matter and cannot be ignored, but they do not cement a legacy. Over time, they fade.

To his team, leadership felt like box-checking rather than connection and the cost was significant. Tim lost several high-performing leaders along the way.

One of them was Diane. She was a strong leader and the likely successor to his role. She tried repeatedly to help Tim see another dimension of leadership: one rooted in compassion, presence, and people. Despite her efforts, Tim refused to shift. Eventually, Diane left the organization, leaving behind a leadership void that no metric could fill.

Leadership moments like that often go unnoticed until it's too late.

Other moments arrive quietly; reminders of what's possible when someone chooses to believe in another person before they believe in themselves. One of those moments began with Fran in a smaller healthcare setting.

Fran worked in a department tangled in disarray. The culture was cliquish, communication was poor, and chaos had become normalized. She felt disconnected and unseen. Fran shared thoughtful ideas to improve morale and collaboration, but her manager and supervisors dismissed them with familiar phrases: *We tried that before. That won't work here.* Long tenure had stalled innovation and silenced new thinking.

Over time, discouragement took its toll. Fran began searching for opportunities elsewhere, convinced there had to be something better.

Still, she regularly stopped into my human resource office. At first, conversations were casual. Over time, they became deeper and more reflective. Beneath years of frustration and self-doubt, I saw something Fran couldn't yet see; quiet brilliance, insight, resilience, and untapped leadership potential.

An unofficial mentorship began to form. Listening became the priority. I offered a few gentle nudges, asked thoughtful questions, and most importantly, I held up a mirror to the strengths Fran had long overlooked.

Slowly, things began to change. Her posture softened. She made more eye contact. Her smile returned. Her voice, which was once tentative, became more confident and direct.

Alone on the Island

One afternoon, Fran walked in and shared that she had received a job offer. She was torn. Leaving promised relief from dysfunction but staying held a possibility she couldn't quite name. She felt alone. Misplaced. Caught between comfort and courage.

I shared a truth learned many times over the years: Sometimes you need to stand alone to discover what you're truly capable of.

That metaphorical island of self-discovery, away from the noise, validation, and opinions of others, can be a gift. It creates space to reflect, to uncover hidden strengths and time to choose a path on your own terms.

I had to resist the urge to rush in to rescue Fran, I just needed to be present so she could find her own footing knowing she had support if she needed it.

Fran didn't need a push; she just needed someone to believe in her long enough for her to believe in herself. She chose to stay. Through my advocacy, I helped secure her a spot in a year-long leadership development program.

Fran began to see what had been there right along: grit, grace, intelligence, and untapped leadership potential. She applied for internal roles that stretched her and grew quickly. Years later, she shared, *"You saw through all my layers. You believed in me before I believed in myself."*

Today, Fran is a thriving Vice President. And she now mentors others with the same care and conviction that once helped her rise.

Mentorship Under the Iceberg

Mentorship often lives beneath the surface.

Like an iceberg, what's visible is only a fraction of its power. The most meaningful mentorship happens below the waterline, unseen by most. It can look like:

- Listening without jumping in to fix the situation
- Asking reflective questions without giving the answers
- Naming their strengths out loud
- Advocating behind closed doors

It isn't about big gestures; it is about being a consistent presence. One investment can lead to an exponential impact.

The Courage to Be Seen

Being vulnerable at work is difficult, especially when it feels like no one is in your corner. Mentors change that. They help uncover the strengths hidden beneath survival mode. They name the talent you've been too afraid to claim. And they walk beside you while you're still figuring it out.

Sometimes, all you need is one person to say: *"I see you. You're ready. Let the world see you, too."*

Reflection Prompt

- Who believed in you before you believed in you? What did they help you see?
- Who in your life or workplace might be waiting for someone to call out their brilliance?

12

Empowered on Purpose: Owning Your Own Growth

---

*How confidence, clarity, and accountability transform
how you show up for yourself and others*

Empowerment Is a Mirror

SOMETIMES RESISTANCE ISN'T a lack of motivation, it's fear.
Fear of failure.
Fear of not being enough.
Fear of being exposed.

Fear has a way of triggering instinctive reactions: fight, flight, or hide.

I'm reminded of walking the boardwalk at the National Seashore in Cape Cod. As you approach the water, fiddler crabs line both sides of the wooden path. The moment you step forward, they disappear, burying themselves in the sand until only small holes remain. Their response to a perceived threat is immediate and automatic.

The workplace isn't much different.

When threats, real or imagined, show up, people react the same way. They run, they fight or they hide. The work of empowerment begins by noticing those reactions and getting curious about what's driving them. Unpacking fear is often the first step toward growth.

Empowerment doesn't eliminate fear. Instead, it fills the space between fear and potential with belief, direction, and accountability.

And when that balance clicks, something shifts.

That's when growth happens.
That's when you begin to see yourself differently.
That's when empowerment becomes real.

Empowerment shows up when you lead with **confidence:** feeling grounded and capable; **clarity,** knowing where you're going; and **accountability,** choosing action over avoidance, especially when things feel uncomfortable.

You'll know it when you feel it.

Empowerment doesn't always arrive with fireworks. More often, it reveals itself quietly; in how you carry yourself, how you think, and how you respond to the world around you.

Ask yourself: *What do I look like when I'm empowered?*

Does any of this sound familiar?

- You make decisions without excessive second-guessing or needing approval
- You view conflict as an opportunity for growth rather than something to avoid

- You take risks, try new approaches, and stretch beyond your comfort zone
- You reframe failure as feedback, not a label
- You see situations with broader perspective and deeper clarity
- You stop minimizing problems or catastrophizing them; you assess, respond, and move forward

That's the look and feel of empowerment.

It isn't heavy; it doesn't trap you; it doesn't keep you stuck.

Empowerment is energy.

It's that fire in the belly belief that you're capable of more, and willing to act on it.

But let's be clear: empowerment isn't something you're given. It's something you choose.

You invest in yourself.
You believe in your capacity to grow.
You get honest about your gaps and you take responsibility for closing them.

When your energy is tied up in resistance, pushing back against change or deflecting responsibility, you're not empowered. You're stuck.

Great leaders understand this. They know empowerment can't be forced or handed down. It has to come from within. What leaders *can* do is create the conditions for empowerment. These environments are where people feel seen, safe, challenged, and supported.

The "Spaghetti Effects"

I've seen this pattern repeatedly in employee relations: when confidence is low, accountability becomes slippery.

Excuses start flying—like spaghetti thrown at the wall—hoping something sticks.
It's the system.
No one trained me.
That's not my job.

Strong leaders don't play that game.

When excuses surface, the work is to stay calm and grounded. Accountability becomes a game of catch. You return the ball—firmly, kindly, and consistently.

This isn't about punishment.
It's about momentum.

When leaders allow excuses to linger, they unintentionally enable avoidance. But when accountability is held clearly and compassionately, something powerful happens.

People either step up… or step out.

And either outcome brings clarity.

Reflection Prompts

- What do you look like when you're at your most empowered?
- How do you speak, decide, lead, and respond in that version of yourself?
- What would it take to show up that way more often?

Empowered on Purpose isn't just a concept. It's a choice; one that requires reflection and action. When those two come together, real growth begins.

13

Brave Enough to Pivot

The Confidence Reset

Have you ever felt stuck, like you've outgrown your current role or that invisible walls are closing in? That restless feeling may be your inner voice whispering that it's time for a change.

Being bold doesn't always mean walking away. Sometimes it means stretching where you are, taking on new responsibilities, volunteering for a project that scares you a little, or expanding your role in ways that reignite your growth. Other times, being bold means taking a leap, pursuing an advanced degree, pivoting industries, or starting over somewhere new.

Each bold move carries risk, but it also carries the promise of reward. Growth demands courage, the courage to trust yourself enough to take the first step before you can see the whole staircase.

When Change Finds You

Career paths rarely unfold in a straight line. Career transitions don't always arrive wrapped in opportunity. Sometimes transitions come by choice; other times, they arrive unexpectedly: a layoff, a leadership change, a department closure or a closed door. In those moments of vulnerability, it can be hard to imagine being bold when the identity you've spent years building feels shaken.

But this is precisely when confidence must lead the way. Take inventory of your skills, achievements, and lessons learned. Each success and setback has taught you something valuable. Those experiences form the foundation for what's next. When you pause to reflect, you begin to see new opportunities that weren't visible before.

When Self-Doubt Tries to Steer the Wheel

After more than two decades of sitting in corporate boardrooms, coaching executive leaders, and guiding graduate students, I have witnessed a quiet pattern showing up repeatedly, even among the most brilliant professionals. Confidence wavers. Self-doubt creeps in. And for women especially, imposter syndrome whispers, *"You don't belong here."*

Watching extraordinary leaders question their promotions, second-guess why they were selected for advanced programs, or doubt whether they truly belonged in an MBA classroom, despite every credential, every achievement, and every earned moment that got them there.

Here's the truth that matters most: you earned your place. You didn't land where you are by luck, timing, or accident. You prepared, you showed up, and you did the work. Confidence isn't arrogance, it's the calm recognition of your own capability.

When doubt tries to steer the wheel, resist the urge to shrink, apologize, or play small. Trust that you are ready, even if you don't feel ready yet. Growth happens not in the absence of doubt, but in the decision to move forward despite it.

The Power of Shared Strength

One of the most remarkable transformations I have witnessed happens inside leadership programs dedicated for women in STEM (Science, Technology, Engineering and Mathematics) fields; brilliant, high-performing executives from around the world who arrive on a Sunday evening carrying so much more than luggage. Many have never met, yet they walk in with similar stories: the pressure to excel in male-dominated industries, the exhaustion of balancing demanding careers with personal responsibilities, and the quiet, lingering question of whether they truly belong.

On that first night, they are often guarded, unsure, and cautious measuring their words, protecting their confidence, wondering if everyone else has it more figured out than they do. But over the course of four days, something extraordinary unfolds. The masks fall away, the shoulders lower, the laughter gets louder. They share fears, successes, insecurities, and aspirations. In shared vulnerability, they find strength.

In recognizing each other's fears, they reclaim their own confidence. They laugh, cry, and connect deeply. They leave not only better equipped professionally, but lifted personally, not just as colleagues, but as allies.

When women have spaces to show up authentically, they rise, not just individually, but collectively.

Finding Confidence in the Overwhelm

This same transformation occurs in graduate students who juggle full-time jobs, family obligations, and demanding coursework. In those early weeks, the pressure can feel suffocating, like there's no air left to breathe.

When students come to me feeling defeated, I remind them: *You are not failing, you are stretching.* Growth feels uncomfortable because you are building capacity. Together, we work on letting go of what doesn't matter, focusing on what does, and finding grace amid the chaos.

I'll never forget one student who was nine months pregnant during her final capstone. She worked full time, cared for a toddler, and still completed her project days after giving birth. Despite her exhaustion, she radiated determination. Confidence isn't about perfection, it's about perseverance. Her story is proof that confidence grows when you keep showing up, even when it's hard.

To grow into who you're becoming, you must quiet the old stories of fear and make space for resilience, grace, and self-belief.

Leading Through the Unknown

If you've just been promoted, your new team is watching, testing and waiting to see who you'll be. You may feel uncertain in your leadership skin, but authenticity is your greatest ally. Be yourself, even if it feels clumsy at first.

Leading a new or dysfunctional team requires patience and persistence. Early on, focus on listening and understanding before making changes. You'll uncover what's working, what's broken, and who's ready to grow.

Inheriting a divided team filled with conflict, excuses, and blurred roles revealed an important truth: turning things around requires time, honesty, and tenacity. Some individuals chose to move on, new talent stepped in, and trust slowly began to rebuild, brick by brick, decision by decision.

There were no perfect answers along the way. Mistakes were made. Growth was required by everyone. And through that process, a powerful lesson emerged: learning agility, the ability to keep moving forward even without a clear roadmap is the real differentiator. It's what separates leaders who simply manage from leaders who transform.

Being bold isn't about fearlessness, it's about faith. Faith that even when the path isn't clear, you can navigate the unknown.

Be bold. Be brave. Be you.
The next chapter of your story begins when you decide to turn the page.

Confidence isn't something you find once; it's something you continue to build upon, rebuild, moment by moment, through action, reflection, and courage.

Remember: progress isn't always loud. Sometimes it's the quiet act of believing in yourself enough to begin.

Self-doubt will visit; that's part of being human. But it doesn't get to unpack and stay.

You have overcome more than you remember, achieved more than you acknowledge, and grown more than you give yourself credit for.

You are capable. You are ready. You belong.

The world doesn't need a perfect version of you. It needs the confident one who keeps showing up.

14

The Power of Your Peer Table

Why Your Most Valuable Team Isn't the One You Lead

YOU'VE POURED TIME, energy, and intention into building a loyal, high-performing team. You've hired the right people, coached through growing pains, and celebrated milestones together. That team has become a source of pride, and rightly so. But here's a leadership truth that often surprises even the most seasoned leaders:

The most important team in your organization is not the one you lead.
It's the one you're *on*, your peer team.

Yes, your direct reports are critical. Yes, their success is deeply tied to your own. But when the peer team—the group of leaders tasked with setting direction, solving cross-functional challenges, and modeling organizational culture—fails to connect or align, everything beneath it begins to crack.

Let me tell you about Mike.

Mike was an exceptional director in a community-facing role. He was passionate, driven, and effective at building external partnerships in community relations. But each week, when the organization's director's team gathered for their strategic 90-minute meetings, Mike was missing.

He would make an excuse that he had another obligation, it was part of his job to be in the community. And for a while, people understood. But over time, the team grew frustrated. Everyone else showed up—fully present—while Mike operated as if his work lived in its own silo. The perception grew that he wasn't invested in internal strategy. Worse, it signaled that he didn't value his peers.

Eventually, the team reached a tipping point. His continued absence and refusal to engage fractured trust. Despite his external wins, Mike's inability to contribute internally led to a demotion, and his eventual departure.

Mike didn't fail because he wasn't skilled. He failed because he didn't value the peer table.

In leadership, one of the most underestimated causes of derailment is this: **not building strong peer relationships.**

Peers are the ones who influence the broader culture. They're your allies in decision-making, your mirrors when blind spots show up, and your collaborators in building something that lasts beyond your own team.

Ask yourself:

- Do I consistently show up for my peer team?
- Am I known for being dependable in shared leadership spaces?
- How am I contributing to a culture of collaboration over competition?

Leadership is not a solo sport. And your most valuable currency isn't just the team that reports to you; it's the trust you build among those seated next to you at the table.

Coaching Questions: The Power of Your Peer Table

Self-Awareness

1. How do I currently show up in peer meetings or cross-functional leadership settings?
2. What might my peer team say about my level of engagement or collaboration?
3. Do I prioritize my peer team the way I prioritize my direct reports?

Relationship Building

4. What intentional actions have I taken to build trust with my peers?
5. When conflict arises on my peer team, how do I typically respond?
6. Do I view my peers as allies, competitors, or something in between?

Commitment to Team Goals

7. Am I contributing to the strategic vision of the organization *beyond* my department?
8. How do I support or hinder team accountability across the peer group?
9. Have I ever opted out (intentionally or not) of important conversations? Why?

Course Correction

10. Where have I fallen short in being a fully engaged peer, and what am I willing to do to rebuild?
11. What boundaries or beliefs do I need to shift to make space for deeper peer collaboration?
12. What specific behavior will I commit to that reinforces my accountability *to* and *with* my peers?

Next Steps

13. Who on my peer team do I need to connect with or re-connect with?
14. What can I do at the next team meeting to model shared leadership?
15. How will I measure my success in showing up for *this* team, not just the one I lead?

15

From Contributor to Catalyst

Making the Leap from Doing the Work to Leading the Way

You walk into work and immediately sense something has shifted. A leadership change has occurred, and before you can process what it means, you're called aside and congratulated on your promotion. You smile, taking in the words, but beneath the excitement, a wave of uncertainty rises.

You were great at your job—reliable, efficient, results-driven. You knew the work and owned it. But this? This is new terrain. What lies ahead isn't just a new title, it's a transformation.

Becoming a manager isn't a reward for past performance; it's an invitation to evolve. The very strengths that earned your promotion—technical expertise, independence, speed—aren't the same ones that will make you successful now. Leadership requires a new mindset, new skills, and a new definition of success.

The Peer-to-Boss Transition

One of the hardest parts of leadership is stepping into authority among those who once saw you as a peer. Yesterday, you were joining them for lunch, after-work drinks, and weekend get-togethers. Today, you're lucky to get a polite "good morning."

What changed? You did. You're now responsible for performance, accountability, and direction. That shift can feel isolating and it will test you. Some will see how far they can push, leaning on your old friendship. Others might ask for special treatment or expect you to look the other way.

This is where leadership begins, with boundaries. Assume the role you've been entrusted with. It may feel uncomfortable at first to hold the line on expectations, but over time, those around you will understand. Friendships may not look the same, but what you'll gain is something deeper: respect. Just don't be surprised if the Friday night invites stop coming.

Letting Go to Grow

The toughest habit for new managers to break is holding on to their old job. Without letting go, you'll find yourself doing two jobs: yours and theirs. You'll keep solving the same problems, completing the same tasks, and feeling increasingly stretched thin.

And the truth is, your team doesn't need you to do their work. They need you to trust them to do it.

In my 30+ years in Human Resources, I've seen hundreds of new managers step into leadership. Most had the knowledge to manage, but not the emotional readiness to lead. They knew *what* to do, but not always *how* to do it. That's where many get stuck.

Let me tell you about Lucy and when results aren't enough.

Lucy arrived with momentum. She had been hired from outside the company because of her reputation for getting things done. She moved fast, delivered results and didn't waste time on distractions. Leadership trusted her to raise the bar.

On day one, Lucy called her new team together. She set expectations quickly and firmly and told them she was not there to babysit adults. Drama, she made clear, would not be tolerated.

What she didn't do was pause.

She didn't observe the team dynamic or meet the people one on one. She wasn't interested in asking questions or listening to context. She set a negative tone before she built trust and the message landed hard.

Within days, employees described her leadership style as "barking orders." Lucy was surprised by the reaction. From her perspective, she was simply being direct. From the team's view, she was issuing commands to people she didn't yet know.

Lucy spent most of her time in her office. Lunch happened behind a closed door. Her introverted nature, combined with her task-driven focus, created distance from the team. They interpreted silence as being disinterested.

Results remained but became stalled. Unfortunately, Lucy was never able to recover from such a poor start. Her emotional intelligence was underdeveloped, particularly in the areas of self-awareness and empathy. She was unwilling to explore her strengths or acknowledge opportunities for growth. Because she was hired into the role, Lucy assumed her success was already proven and that there was little left to learn.

When her leader raised the importance of relationship-building or invited her to seek feedback to address these blind spots, Lucy became defensive. Rather than stepping into the perspective of her team to build empathy and repair strained relationships, she allowed those fractures to widen, ultimately letting them derail her effectiveness as a leader.

It was less than 6 months, and she was asked to leave. While Lucy had excellent technical skills and knew *what* to do as a leader, she ignored *how* leadership works through connection, trust, and inspiring the team to achieve shared goals.

The People Puzzle

It's easy to see why. Most managers lead based on what they've seen before. If you've had strong role models, you're fortunate. If not, you may be leading without a map or worse, leading like your last bad boss!

Managing people isn't like managing systems or spreadsheets. Systems don't have emotions, fears, or stories. People do, and they bring all of that to work with them.

If you look up the word "manager," you'll see verbs like *plan*, *direct*, *monitor*, and *control.* Those work for processes, not people. Your job isn't to control behavior; it's to shape it, develop it, and connect it to something meaningful.

That starts with conversations. Don't wait weeks to address behavior, give feedback, or acknowledge success. Time weakens your message and erodes trust. The sooner you engage respectfully, and directly, the stronger your leadership becomes. Let me tell you about Carol and when timing can change everything.

Carol wasn't disengaged, she was underutilized.

As the front-facing receptionist, she served as the first point of contact for customers, employees and vendors. On slow days, the quiet stretched on. With the kitchen nearby, Carol filled the time by chatting with coworkers as they passed by. The conversations were friendly, harmless, it seemed; until they weren't. When the office got busy, Carol stayed in conversation while the visitors waited. When someone finally approached the reception window, she appeared rushed or worse, annoyed. Complaints surfaced from both internal employees and external visitors.

Her manager knew. Each time the issue came up, he dismissed it. *"That's just Carol"*, he said. By not addressing the behavior, he was reinforcing the bad behavior and approving of it. Time passed and the behavior became a habit. Carol had no idea she was doing anything wrong. When her manager finally raised the issue, the moment had gone stale. The example he used didn't resonate. Carol felt confused and defensive and unclear of how to fix it. Next time, the feedback was timely, specific and balanced. Her manager acknowledged Carol's warmth and friendliness along with outlining expectations for prioritizing the reception window. Together, they discussed how to stay approachable without losing focus.

Carol adjusted immediately and the behavior changed. She was able to be successful and the complaints stopped. Carol felt supported instead of being criticized.

The difference wasn't Carol, it was leadership.

Avoid the Task Trap

When you're new, it's tempting to retreat to the work you know best… the tasks. That's where you feel competent and safe. But you're no longer paid to *do*; you're paid to *lead.*

That means stepping back and learning to see the bigger picture. Ask yourself:

- Am I operating at 10,000 feet, where tasks live?
- Or am I rising to 75,000 feet, where vision, people, and strategy align?

Your growth—and your team's—depends on your willingness to elevate your view.

When I first transitioned into an executive role, I struggled with this shift. Coming from Operations, a good day meant crossing off my long task list. Sitting quietly to think felt unproductive and almost irresponsible. I remember staring at the ceiling, out my window, at charts on my corkboard wondering, *"What am I supposed to be thinking about?"* Then it hit me, I got the A-ha! Leadership wasn't about today anymore. It was about tomorrow, three months from now, a year from now and beyond. To do that, it required dedicated "think time."

Strategic thinking required practice. I put a note onto my computer reminding myself to think ahead. I used the organization's strategic plan as a guardrail to expand my thinking and connect my daily work to longer term goals. This shift helped me to get out of the weeds, see the broader horizon to have a larger impact.

Redefined Success

Great managers don't hoard knowledge or solve every problem. They coach, mentor, and empower. They create space for others to grow, even if it means stepping back.

Leadership isn't about control, it's about influence.

You've moved from managing tasks to cultivating potential, your own and others'.
You've gone from contributor to catalyst.

Now, it's time to lead the way.

Leadership Pause: Rising Above the Task List

Take a few moments to reflect on your own leadership transition:

1. **What part of your old role is hardest to let go of?**
   Identify one task or habit you're still holding onto that could be delegated.
2. **How are you defining success in your new role?**
   Is it still about checking boxes or is it about developing people and creating impact?
3. **What relationships need redefining?**
   Think about one former peer relationship that has shifted. How can you rebuild it with clarity and respect?
4. **At what altitude are you leading today?**
   Picture yourself at 10,000 feet, deep in the tasks. Or at 75,000 feet, focused on vision and growth. What one action could help you rise higher this week?

Leadership Insight:

True leadership begins when you stop managing the work and start inspiring the people doing it.

16

From People Pleaser to Purpose Protector

The courage to say No

CHOOSING A CAREER in Human Resources or Management, roles rooted in service is one of the most rewarding paths you can take. Supporting people, solving problems, and helping create a better workplace for others is meaningful work. But there is a hidden cost to serving others and it's easy to lose yourself in the process.

When your instinct is to care, to help, and to say yes, you may slowly start to put your own needs last. At first, putting yourself last feels selfless, even noble. You tell yourself you're doing it for the team, the organization, the greater good. But over time, constant giving without boundaries begins to erode something important. Resentment creeps in quietly. You start to feel invisible, as though your voice doesn't matter. The work that once energized you begins to feel heavy, less like impact and more like obligation.

People can sense when you're a people pleaser. Without meaning to, they pile on requests, confident you'll find a way to make it all happen. And you do, until the weight becomes too much.

Eventually, the moment comes when you finally speak up, but it doesn't sound like the calm, thoughtful leader others expect. It comes out as frustration. The polished tone is replaced by exhaustion and anger. This is often where burnout shows itself, not as weakness, but as a breaking point.

That breaking point met Amanda head-on.

Amanda was a fixer by nature, both professionally and personally. Her calendar told the story: four children juggling dance, scouts, and sports, deep involvement in school parent organizations, and a life that ran at full capacity with little room to breathe. What looked like commitment from the outside felt like constant obligation on the inside.

At work, Amanda was an exceptional manager. Her team trusted her completely. They came to her with every challenge, every question, every concern, and she took it all on. Each yes felt aligned with her identity as a helpful, supportive leader. But in solving problems for others, she unintentionally enabled behaviors to continue and left herself with less and less time to focus on her own responsibilities.

The weight accumulated quietly, until it didn't. During a senior leadership meeting, Amanda snapped. The moment was out of character, but the consequences were real. She was reprimanded, and more importantly, she realized she had reached the edge of her patience. The cost of carrying everyone else's burdens had begun to show up in her health, her energy, and her sense of self.

Amanda didn't lack commitment or competence. She lacked boundaries.

This chapter isn't about becoming less caring. It's about learning to protect your purpose, so your 'yes' remains meaningful and your 'no' becomes an act of leadership, not guilt.

When "Yes" Becomes Too Costly

Those who struggle to say *no* often overcommit and underdeliver. Not because they lack skill or dedication, but because they're stretched too thin. When this happens, trust begins to erode; trust in your reliability, your consistency, and your ability to deliver on promises.

No one in leadership wakes up wanting to disappoint others. Yet when you constantly say yes, even to things that don't align with your priorities, you set yourself up for burnout and disconnection.

The good news? Boundaries aren't barriers, they're bridges. They connect your purpose to your capacity and ensure your impact is sustainable.

The Juggler's Lens

Think of yourself as a juggler. Each ball in the air represents a commitment, a responsibility, or a promise. Some balls are glass—high priority, high visibility, fragile. If they fall, the consequences are significant. Others are rubber—flexible, forgiving, able to bounce back.

When everything feels urgent, pause and ask yourself:

Which of these balls will break if I drop it?

Focus on the glass ones. Let the rubber ones bounce for now. They'll come back, and you'll catch them on the rebound.

That's what effective prioritization looks like in practice; not doing it all, but doing what matters most.

Redefining "No"

Saying no isn't rejection, it's redirection. It's not resistance; it's responsibility. This can show up everywhere, not just at work. Every time you choose where your time and energy go, you're making a leadership decision, whether you realize it or not.

Sometimes it's personal. A friend who wants you to help them move, but instead of checking your availability, they just set the date and time for you. You don't have to decline outright or silently resent it. You could be pointed in your response with honesty: "I'd like to help you move, I'm available on these two dates and time, let me know what works." You're not saying no, you're setting a boundary that respects both of you.

Other times, it's professional. Your boss adds something new to your already full plate. Rather than absorbing it quietly or pushing back defensively, try reframing the conversation: "Help me understand your top priorities so I can make sure I'm focused on the right things."

That simple shift moves the conversation from obligation to alignment. It signals partnership, thoughtfulness, and a commitment to doing the right work well, not defiance.

Protecting your time protects your performance. Boundaries don't weaken relationships, they strengthen them. When you're clear about what you can take on, you build trust. You will show others that when you say yes, you mean what you say and that you're serious about delivering with intention and excellence.

Protecting Your Calendar (and Your Sanity)

Your calendar reflects your priorities. Guard it fiercely. Continuously triage your calendar and meetings to ensure you schedule time for focus, reflection, and renewal. Build in thinking and planning time. You'll never regret giving yourself the gift of time, it's one of the most powerful tools for clarity and calmness.

**People pleasers protect comfort.
Purpose protectors protect impact.**

Remember:

It's okay to say, "Let me check my capacity before I commit."
It's okay to block time for deep work, planning, or simply thinking.
People pleasers protect comfort. Purpose protectors protect impact.

The "Sara" Lesson

I once coached Sara, a talented Customer Service professional newly promoted to manager. She had deep institutional knowledge and could do nearly any task better than anyone else. At first, she continued doing the work she'd mastered because she could.

But "could" isn't "should."

Within months, Sara was overwhelmed. She was eager to prove herself, so she worked harder, stayed later, and took on more. Eventually, her commitment turned into exhaustion.

Nine months in, her resilience had transformed into resentment. She wasn't failing, she was *over functioning*. What she needed wasn't more effort; it was permission to lead differently.

Leadership requires letting go, delegating with intention, trusting others, and creating space for growth. It means believing in someone enough to let them learn, even when mistakes are part of the process.

Sara, instead of taking the project on herself, chose to assign a stretch opportunity to a capable team member. When progress moved slower than expected, the temptation to step in and take the work back was real. But rather than re-claiming control, Sara stayed engaged in a different way. She offered support, asked thoughtful questions, and coached the employee toward success.

The project was completed, but the real win was what happened along the way. The one team member gained confidence, capability, and ownership. By letting go, Sara chose long-term development over short-term efficiency. And in doing so, she didn't lose momentum, she multiplied it.

Reclaiming Balance: The Balance Blueprint

If you've ever felt off balance, this simple exercise can help you reset.

Instructions:

1. Draw a circle on a sheet of paper.
2. Divide it into sections, like slices of a pie.

3. Label each wedge with what matters most: Work, Family, Health, Friends, Growth, etc.
4. Shade in how fulfilled you feel in each area (10% for unbalanced, 100% for fully balanced).
5. Step away, then return and notice the patterns.
6. Identify one or two areas that need more attention.
7. Commit to one small action in each within the next 30 days.

Writing it down makes it real. Taking small, consistent steps turns imbalance into momentum and momentum into peace.

Saying No to Peers

Your boss isn't the only one who can stretch you too thin, your peers can, too. Sometimes, it's not intentional. A colleague who struggles to say *no* might overcommit and then come to you for a "favor." That favor often turns into something bigger, something they take off their plate and quietly place onto yours. Before you know it, you're juggling their priorities while they breathe a sigh of relief (or worse, take the credit).

Resist the urge to catch the glass balls your peers toss over the wall. Protect your focus and energy. Saying *no* isn't selfish, it's a leadership skill. It shows discernment, boundaries, and respect for your own commitments and is vital to self-care.

Mike and I had a strong working relationship. He'd joined the organization a year before me; smart, capable, and ambitious, but his people leadership skills needed work. He micromanaged his team and struggled to delegate, so when his plate overflowed, he often tried to hand things off to me.

His approach was subtle at first: he'd compliment my strength with the "people stuff" or imply the project really belonged in my area. It was a guilt play disguised as flattery. Despite several polite refusals, he kept pushing.

Mike would say, "You're just so good with people. This part fits your strengths more than mine." I accepted the compliment, "I appreciate that, but this piece sits with you and your team." Mike reiterated, "I know, but you'd move it forward faster, and the team would respond so well to you."

Finally, I stopped cushioning my words. I called it out: directly, clearly, and respectfully. And you know what? It felt empowering. I wasn't being difficult; I was drawing a boundary. And that moment taught me something invaluable: protecting your time is not about saying *no* to people, it's about saying *yes* to what truly matters.

When you need to decline, be clear, direct, and unapologetic. You don't owe anyone a lengthy explanation or justification. Try one of these confident responses:

- "I'm dedicating my time to other priorities right now and can't take that on."
- "I'm fully booked with competing deadlines."
- "I need to stay focused on my current commitments."
- "Taking that on would jeopardize the quality of my existing work."
- "I don't have the bandwidth for that right now."
- "I'm not able to give this the attention it deserves."

If you want to offer help *later*, you can delay your response:

- "I can't take this on right now, but I could help with [specific part of the task] once I finish [current project]. Would that work?"

Saying No to Yourself

Through my coaching work, one consistent pattern shows up again and again: high performers almost always find room for one more "yes." When something new and exciting comes along; a project, opportunity, or challenge, it can feel irresistible. It looks like growth, visibility, and momentum. But that same instinct to stretch can also lead to burnout if it's not balanced with self-honesty.

Jill didn't hesitate when the new opportunity surfaced. She was a capable leader overseeing product development and in the middle of rebuilding a team after years of poor leadership. Her mandate was already significant: turnaround results, hire and train new staff, and develop a successor. Then came the chance to launch an entirely new line of business.

Jill had prior experience that gave her a clear edge over other candidates. She saw the upside immediately and this could catapult her to the next level. Confident and persuasive, she influenced her boss and key stakeholders to give her the opportunity.

What she didn't do was pause to fully map the scope of what she was taking on.

Because the business line was new, there was little internal expertise to draw from. Jill would need to source external talent, bring them up to speed, and prepare the team for launch on top of her existing responsibilities. She could see the finish line, but not the full terrain between where she stood and where she was headed.

Months of long hours followed. The strain began to show. Jill stopped sleeping well and found herself getting sick more often. Meanwhile, the team she had been charged with rebuilding started to feel the impact. One-on-one meetings were postponed or replaced with back-to-back sessions for the new venture. Mistakes increased and metrics slipped.

Without realizing it, Jill had taken her eye off the team that was counting on her most.

She wasn't failing because she lacked capability or commitment. She was failing because she had said yes too much, and no to herself. In the end, she couldn't lead both responsibilities well. Letting one "yes" go might have protected the work, the people, and herself.

This was a familiar lesson for me.

Six months into developing a talent acquisition strategy, building a new team, and creating tools to strengthen organizational Recruiting, I was in a groove. Things were clicking. We were achieving results and collaborating beautifully. Having led entire HR departments before, focusing on one function felt manageable, even easy.

Then came my mistake.

In a one-on-one meeting, I casually told my boss that I'd probably be bored in six months. Be careful what you put out into the universe! Within three months, my role expanded dramatically. I was suddenly leading a new discipline, managing a struggling team, and trying to build infrastructure from the ground up all at once.

I became buried. The hours stretched longer, and the pressure mounted. I had to hire the right people, reset priorities, and keep the department afloat. In the end, it *was* a growth experience but it came at a cost.

Looking back, I learned that every "yes" should come with a pause for reflection. Understand the true scope of what you're about to take on. Identify what support and resources you'll need to be successful. Most importantly, ask yourself whether this opportunity will elevate your impact or quietly drain your energy and joy.

When you want to say *yes*, pause first. Be real with yourself. Sometimes, saying *no* means saying *no* to *you*; to your ambition, curiosity, or desire to please. Before you commit, ask:

- Will this opportunity energize or drain me?
- Do I have the resources and bandwidth to do it well?
- Will this help or hinder my current goals?

A "yes" that pushes you past your limits isn't a growth opportunity; it's a detour into exhaustion.

The Gift of Boundaries

In management and leadership, we're wired to serve. But you can't pour from an empty cup. The most impactful professionals **aren't** the ones who do everything, they're the ones who do the necessary tasks, with intention and energy.

Saying no isn't selfish, it's how you make room for your best YES.

Boundaries don't limit your influence; they expand it. When you protect your time, energy, and wellbeing, you create the space to serve others more powerfully and sustainably.

Saying no isn't selfish, it's how you make room for your best YES.

Leadership Pause

Take a breath.
Reflect on where your energy is going and whether it aligns with where you want it to go. Sometimes the hardest person to say "no" to is yourself. Ambition is powerful, but so is discernment. Every time you pause before saying yes, you're practicing sustainable leadership.

Coaching Reflections:

1. What motivates my "yes"? Is it excitement, fear of missing out, or pressure to please?
2. Where in your personal or professional life do you keep saying *yes* when you really mean *no*?
3. What does a "healthy yes" look like for me?
4. What criteria could I use to decide whether a new opportunity truly aligns with my goals?
5. Where might saying *no* actually create more space for meaningful growth?
6. How can I model healthy boundaries for others who look to me for guidance?

Take a few minutes to journal your answers. Awareness is the first step toward reclaiming your time and energy.

Commit to one small boundary you will honor this week: whether it's declining a nonessential meeting, blocking time to think, or asking for clarity before accepting a new project.

Take time to journal, reflect, or even talk through these questions with a trusted colleague or friend. The goal isn't to limit your ambition, it's to channel it with intention.

Remember, leadership isn't measured by how much you carry. It's defined by how clearly you choose what matters most.

"Boundaries are the courage to love yourself enough to honor your limits."

17

From Manager to Mentor

Building Trust, Accountability, and Growth Through Meaningful One-on-Ones

Redefining the One-on-One: A New Manager's Imperfect but Impactful Journey

MANY NEWLY PROMOTED managers struggle to grasp the purpose and power of one-on-one meetings. It's completely normal to feel awkward at first, some even describe it as "clunky" or "squishy." But with intention and consistency, this simple practice becomes one of your most valuable leadership tools.

If you've never experienced an effective one-on-one yourself, don't worry, it's a skill you can learn. The key is to start early in your leadership journey, set the tone, and prioritize the relationship. These meetings may begin as task-driven "data dumps," but they should evolve into two-way conversations focused on progress, challenges, and development.

Early on, a one-on-one might sound like:

- *"Here's what I worked on this week."*
- *"Here's what I am going to focus on next week."*
- *"Here's where I'm stuck and need your help."*

That's normal… and necessary. But as trust grows, the conversation should deepen. Effective one-on-ones create space for questions like:

- *"What's energizing you right now?"*
- *"Where are you feeling stretched or not gaining momentum?"*
- *"What support do you need from me?"*
- *"What skills or competencies do you want to build upon?"*

The shift happens when the meeting stops being a status update and becomes a thinking space. A place where employees can reflect out loud, test ideas, surface concerns early, and feel seen beyond their task list.

A word of caution: one-on-one time is not for unloading your own stress or to-do list. As a manager, this time belongs to your team. Make space for them. Schedule it. Honor it. Be present.

Effective one-on-ones are:

- Consistent (they may get moved, but not cancelled)
- Curious (more questions than answers)
- Development-focused (not just task-focused)
- Employee-owned (they set the agenda, not the manager)

Making One-on-Ones Work: Practical Tips for Managers

What Great One-on-Ones Look Like:

- Scheduled consistently and treated as non-negotiable
- Free from distractions—phones down, laptops closed
- Focused equally on short-term needs and long-term development

Suggested Format:

- Ask employees to come prepared with a one-page status update
- Include their top 3 focus areas, short/long-term project updates, and progress benchmarks (e.g., 25%, 50%, etc.)
- Highlight key obstacles, issues, or roadblocks for discussion

Development Shouldn't Wait:

Make room—ideally once a month—for intentional developmental conversations. These are your chances to invest in future potential and align on growth.

Performance Conversations: Start With Curiosity

One-on-ones are a chance to reinforce what's working and identify what needs attention. Encourage reflection and dialogue by asking thoughtful, open-ended questions like:

- What's getting in the way of peak performance?
- If fear weren't a factor, what would you do differently?
- What one thing would you change about your role?
- What skills do you want more support or exposure to?
- What do you need from me that you're not getting?

These conversations help employees feel seen and supported, and give you insight into how to lead more effectively.

Development as a Shared Responsibility

Career development isn't a solo journey. While the employee owns their growth, you create the platform. That means creating space, providing guidance, and challenging them to stretch beyond their current role.

Development Planning Framework:

- **Identify 2–3 competency areas** for growth together
- Integrate development into project work or stretch assignments
- Balance learning experiences:
    - 70% through on-the-job learning
    - 20% via mentoring or exposure to others
    - 10% through formal courses or seminars

Questions to Guide Your Thinking as a Manager:

- Can this employee handle greater responsibility?
- What roles could they grow into over the next 1–2 levels?
- Are they better suited to leadership or a specialized expert track?
- What developmental gaps exist: skills or competencies?
- What stretch opportunities can I delegate that would benefit them?
- Am I letting go of authority to empower their growth?
- Am I helping them connect the dots, see trends, and envision the future?

Build Accountability into Every Conversation

Performance and development efforts need accountability to be meaningful. Mutually agree on *what* will be done and *by when*. The "how" belongs to the employee; your job is to support, not control.

Final Thought

Strong one-on-ones are built on trust, presence, and mutual respect. While the process may feel uncertain at first, stick with it. Over time, these conversations will become your greatest tool for inspiring performance, developing talent, and creating lasting impact as a leader.

Why One-on-Ones Matter

New managers often feel unsure about how to run effective one-on-one meetings. Maybe they've never experienced a good one themselves or maybe it just feels awkward at first. That's okay. This is a learnable skill, and it's one of the most powerful tools you have to engage your team, grow talent, and build trust.

Key Principles

Start Early: Set the tone within your first few weeks as a manager.

- **Be Consistent**: Schedule meetings regularly and don't cancel.
- **Be Present**: Your team deserves your full attention—limit distractions.

- **Balance**: Mix tactical check-ins with developmental conversations.
- **Support Growth**: Create space for employees to share goals and obstacles.

Accountability in Action

Always align with *what* will be done and *by when*. Build accountability into your performance and development conversations.

18

Coaching vs. Counseling: Unlocking Performance with the Right Approach

Knowing When to Guide, When to Correct, and How to Bring Out the Best in Your Team

MOST ORGANIZATIONS, ESPECIALLY non-union environments, have some form of progressive discipline policy in place. Understanding the distinction between *coaching* and *counseling* is essential for any leader looking to effectively support and develop their team.

Counseling: Correcting Performance Issues

Counseling is appropriate when an employee is not meeting expectations, and course correction is necessary. This process is not about punishment; it's about clearly identifying the issue, agreeing on what needs to change, establishing a timeline for improvement, and defining what will happen if the behavior does not change.

Example:
Jack has arrived at least 30 minutes late for 4 out of his last 5 scheduled shifts. The goal is for Jack to report on time for each shift. Start by exploring potential barriers: is there something preventing him from arriving on time? Once that's clarified, set a clear expectation: he is responsible for being punctual. If this correction doesn't occur consistently, outline the next step in the progressive discipline process and follow through as necessary.

Coaching: Enhancing Potential

Coaching, on the other hand, is for employees who are already meeting expectations but have the potential to do even more. It's about fine-tuning their performance, encouraging growth, and preparing them for greater responsibilities.

Example:
Anna is efficient and productive in leading peer-level meetings but tends to dominate the conversation. To help her grow, offer coaching on how to facilitate broader participation, perhaps by asking more open-ended questions or creating space for others to contribute. These small tweaks can dramatically improve her impact and confidence as a leader.

Open-ended questions: Here are some examples that yield more than a yes/no response. Typically beginning with "What" or "How".

Reflective Questions:

1. How do you think your peers experience your facilitation style in meetings?
2. What do you notice about who speaks up most—and least—during your meetings?

3. When have you seen a meeting go especially well in terms of balanced participation? What contributed to that?

Exploratory Questions:

4. What strategies have you tried to encourage input from quieter team members? How did they work?
5. What might be some signals that others want to contribute but aren't getting the chance?
6. How do you decide when to share your perspective versus creating space for others to speak first?

Growth-Oriented Questions:

7. What would a more inclusive and engaging meeting look like to you?
8. How might shifting your role from contributor to facilitator change the group dynamic?
9. What's one small change you could try in your next meeting to open space for more voices?

These questions encourage self-awareness, experimentation, and practical action, key ingredients for leadership development.

Key Questions to Guide Your Approach

Before deciding whether to coach or counsel, ask yourself:

1. **Is the behavior observable and measurable?**
    You need clear, specific evidence—not vague impressions.
2. **Does the employee understand what's expected?**
    Clarity is foundational to accountability.

3. **Has the employee received the proper training?**
   Sometimes underperformance is a result of gaps in knowledge, not motivation.
4. **Has the employee previously been rewarded for underperformance?**
   Mixed messages or overlooked behaviors can undermine accountability.
5. **Is the issue one of ability or willingness?**
   Identify whether the challenge is skill-based or motivational; this distinction shapes your response.

By knowing when to coach and when to counsel, you position yourself as a thoughtful, effective leader; someone who not only addresses issues but also unlocks potential in others.

19

Feedback is a Gift: Honest Conversations, Real Growth

How to Embrace, Deliver, and Receive Feedback to Strengthen Trust and Drive Performance

FEEDBACK IS ONE of the greatest tools a leader has, and it truly is a gift. When given and received with intention, feedback can elevate performance, build trust, and deepen professional relationships. But it requires consistency, courage, and vulnerability.

I learned this firsthand when I made feedback part of my regular rhythm with my direct reports. At first, they didn't take it seriously. The responses were playful; one person even asked me to *start* bringing lobster salad on Fridays. But as they saw me integrating their suggestions into meaningful changes, the tone shifted. They realized this wasn't a passing phase; it was an invitation to shape how we worked together. Also, once that trust was established, the feedback became more open, honest, and powerful.

For example, most of my team were introverted. During staff meetings, when decisions were on the table, they often asked for more information before committing. At first, this slowed momentum and created frustration, both for other team members and—if I'm honest—for me as well.

When a team member gave me feedback that they felt rushed and put on the spot, I adjusted my approach. I began sharing materials in advance, giving them time to think, prepare questions, and form clear perspectives.

The result was unexpected: meetings became more efficient, decisions came faster, and confidence increased. By meeting people where they were, we didn't lose momentum. We gained alignment.

One of the most effective frameworks I've used is **Start, Stop, Continue**. It's simple, direct, and non-threatening. It can be used to gather feedback for yourself, to facilitate peer feedback within a team, or to help individuals reflect on how to better support one another.

Start, Stop, Continue Framework

Start:
What's one thing this person could begin doing to enhance team experience or grow their skills?

- What new behavior would improve collaboration or impact?
- Is there a skill they could begin developing?

Stop:
What's one behavior that may be holding them or the team back?

- What actions are ineffective or disruptive?
- What should they stop doing to help the team succeed?

Continue:
What's working well that they should build on?

- What strengths have made them effective?
- What behaviors contribute positively to the team or project?

Tip: Start with "Continue." It's less threatening and reinforces what's already going well, building a foundation of safety before moving into areas of improvement.

Receiving Feedback with Grace

When you ask for feedback, you need to model how to receive it well. That means resisting the urge to get defensive: verbally, physically, or emotionally. Feedback isn't always easy to hear, but it's crucial to understand the "why" behind what's being shared.

I'll admit, I was caught off guard the first time I was told to *stop* something. A colleague asked me to stop listening to voicemails on speakerphone, it was disrupting her focus. It seemed small, but to her, it mattered. And if I hadn't asked, I never would've known. That moment, and others like it, taught me that small changes often create the biggest shifts in team dynamics.

Giving Feedback: Hitting the Bullseye

Giving feedback can feel uncomfortable. Leaders sometimes hesitate because they want to be liked, avoid conflict, or simply don't know how to do it effectively. But giving clear, actionable feedback is a non-negotiable part of leadership.

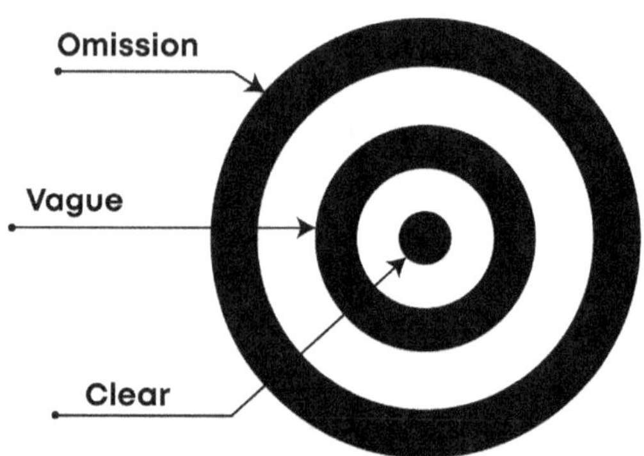

Think of feedback like aiming at a target:

- **Outer Ring – Omission:**
  The issue is avoided or vaguely referenced. The conversation might feel like a friendly chat, but the actual behavior isn't addressed. The message is lost.
- **Middle Ring – Vague:**
  The leader tries to soften the feedback with the "compliment sandwich" (what some call the "spank and thank" approach). It leaves employees unclear about what really needs to change.
- **Bullseye – Clear, Constructive, and Collaborative:**
  The message is direct and focused. The employee understands what the issue is, how it affects the team, and what specific change is needed. You ask questions to reach mutual understanding and encourage accountability. You don't own their behavior, they do. Your job is

to provide the platform and tools for their success, not carry the weight of their performance.

When Feedback is Met with Resistance

It's not uncommon for employees to push back. That's okay; resistance is part of growth. Refer to the chart to help you prepare for and respond to common forms of pushback.

Remember: giving and receiving feedback well is a leadership muscle. The more you practice, the stronger it becomes. Create a culture where feedback is normalized, welcomed, and used to elevate everyone's potential, including your own.

Behavior	Sounds like...	Tactics
Angry Defensive	• Loud, yelling, combative • Excuses	• Let the employee vent for a short period, if not too aggressive • Acknowledge the emotion; *"I can see your angry/upset"* • Actively listen and ask open-ended questions to understand the core of the resistance (what, how, tell me about) • Decide if the conversation needs to be postponed (too heated or upset) to continue • Demonstrate sincerity; express support *"I want to see you be successful here"*
Blame Victim Mentality	• "It's not me, it's ___" • I was never told about… • You never trained me in that • I can't do it	• Actively listen for fears - fear of failure, fear of not being good enough; reinforce that you believe in them • Remove the obstacles getting in their way; focus employee on their behavior separating that from who they are • Place the accountability back on the employee; *"Tell me what you can do, not what you can't"* • Offer support by focusing on a previous win to reinforce what they can do
Avoiding	• Silence, no pushback or comments	• Employee may avoid further discussion • Probe with open-ended questions to engage; *"what are your thoughts?"* • Further engagement: asking them, *"What do you need to help you be successful?"*

20

Beyond the Résumé

Unlocking Potential by Hiring for Mindset, Not Just Skill

HIRING FOR ATTITUDE and training for skill is more than a catchy phrase, it's a strategy that builds teams that last. That belief became a living experiment every semester in the leadership courses where students were challenged to debate it. Two groups: one defending attitudes, the other skill and they went head-to-head.

The debates were always spirited, especially when they had to argue against their own beliefs. It was an intentional exercise to get the students thinking about leadership. Leadership demands the willingness to challenge assumptions. Skills can be taught, but a poor attitude is difficult to coach, and even harder to change.

Attitude can be subtle, subjective, and easily disguised in an interview. Yet it always shows up in behavior. That's why defining the traits and actions that signal the right or wrong mindset is essential, and why those traits must be intentionally sought out during the hiring process.

I learned these lessons the hard way, more than once.

Years ago, a recruiter position on my team had turned over for the second time in six months. The previous hire had looked perfect on paper, but their energy told another story. They weren't excited about the work, weren't connecting with candidates, and certainly weren't selling the company with enthusiasm.

This time, it was clear that mindset—not résumé bullet points—had to take priority.

That's when Chris came to mind, a woman I first met years earlier at a leadership training. She was just starting out in her career, but her spark stood out. Curious. Motivated. Warm. There had been casual check-ins after the training over the next few years, and I remembered that she felt unfulfilled in her payroll role. It was a chance for me to outreach on LinkedIn to open the door.

Chris had almost no talent acquisition experience, but she excelled through the interview process. The entire panel selected her as the top choice, except the department VP, who hesitated because of her lack of experience. Without hesitation, I made a promise:
"Let me train her. She will be exceptional."

The VP raised an eyebrow and replied, half-joking and half-serious:
"If this doesn't work, I'll expect your resignation."

Challenge accepted.

Our daily coaching sessions followed for months—covering philosophy, process, tactics, and strategy. Chris absorbed everything, applied feedback instantly, and refined her craft every single day. Within a year, she wasn't just competent, she was thriving. She built strong relationships with hiring managers, consistently brought in quality candidates, and became a trusted partner to the business. Chris' drive and fire in the belly already existed, all she needed was an opportunity.

But not every hiring decision turns into a success story.

Earlier in my career journey, law school had been the plan until a court internship revealed that the work behind the scenes didn't create any spark. New ambitions formed, leading to my first management role at a retail store. It was October, peak holiday season, and the stockroom was overflowing. I needed to hire people immediately.

Corners were cut. The job was posted, walk-ins were funneled over by cashiers, and interviews were done on the spot. One candidate talked a good game and claimed experience. An offer was made instantly, and I left a proud voicemail for the district manager, celebrating such decisive action.

That confidence lasted until 5 p.m.

Mall police walked into the store and asked for the manager. My staff called me to the front when they asked, "Did you hire a guy named Joe today?" I replied "Yes". The mall police then looked at each other before explaining that Joe had a trespassing order against him for harassing several employees at other mall stores.

Then came the part that made my stomach drop. He wasn't even legally allowed on the property.

I was mortified and that didn't begin to cover it. No reference checks. No time taken. My desperation had turned into disaster. The call back to the district manager was one of the hardest. But the lessons from that moment became non-negotiable standards for every hiring decision that followed:

- Never hire on the spot.
- Always check references.
- Invite multiple perspectives into the interview process.
- Don't force fit someone into a role, make sure the role fits them.

Two weeks later, I made a stronger hire, respected the hiring process, trusted my instincts and the team was better for it.

Reflection Question:

Think back to a time when you made a great (or not-so-great) hire. What role did attitude play in that decision and what was the impact over time?
If you had to do it again, what would you look for differently?

Manager Takeaway:

Hiring with Intention: What to Remember

- **Hire for attitude, train for skill.** Technical gaps can be closed with training. A poor attitude will quietly erode your team culture.
- **Pressure creates shortcuts.** Don't let urgency rush you into a bad hire. The time you save today can take you months of recovery later.
- **Check references and use a panel.** Multiple perspectives reduce blind spots and reinforce better decisions.
- **Watch for energy, curiosity, and willingness.** These are often stronger predictors of success than experience alone.
- **If you find someone with heart, invest in them.** Mentorship and training can unlock potential you never saw on a résumé.

21

From Fear to Fuel

How Insecurity Sparked Innovation and Leadership Growth

FEARS HAVE A funny way of showing up, especially when you think they've been buried. They surface unexpectedly especially when you're feeling excluded, unworthy, inauthentic, or afraid to fail. These moments trigger the old internal narratives, the "tapes" that warn, "I'm not good enough, not ready, not credible." If left unexamined, those beliefs quietly influence behavior and can sabotage performance and relationships in the workplace.

The first step to managing fear is acknowledging it which is something rarely easy in the moment.

Early in my career journey, growth came fast. A rapid climb of the corporate ladder led to a Vice President role in Human Resources at a company that didn't produce end products, but populated circuit boards for the medical device industry and others. The workforce was made up of highly skilled engineers and technicians specializing in electronics and soldering.

My responsibility: lead the People strategy and align workforce planning with business goals. Logically, there was no need to master soldering techniques or memorize every component to be effective in the role. But within the first several months, old insecurities resurfaced. It became easy to believe credibility required knowing every technical detail.

So began my grind after hours, pouring over manuals, studying quality standards, shadowing line workers to learn their craft. None of it was required for success. Yet for nearly six months, I approached the role from the weeds, rather than the vantage point required. A leader hired to operate at 100,000 feet was functioning at 10,000 feet and all driven by fear.

The fear was simple but powerful: being found out. Not being good enough. Feeling like an imposter despite an MBA and a solid track record. That quiet fear nearly derailed what I was fully capable of doing well. Even with my education and experience in human resources, I worried my boss, peers, and team wouldn't see me as credible. Most of the leaders around me had years of industry-specific expertise, and I convinced myself that unless I could follow every technical conversation, I didn't belong. In my mind, competence meant knowing everything, right down to soldering.

This is what imposter syndrome sounds like on the inside. The voice isn't loud, but it's relentless, whispering that you must prove your worth rather than trust it. Instead of asking questions or leaning into the strengths I was hired for, I overcompensated. I tried to close a gap that didn't actually exist.

That belief didn't make me stronger. It made me smaller. The cost wasn't just confidence, it was clarity, focus, and energy.

The turning point came with recognition. Once my fear was named, I could manage it. That realization arrived just in time.

The company was growing, but the industry was shrinking. A major local employer had closed and the applicant pool had evaporated. My impossible assignment landed: hire 20 new employees in three months. Every standard tactic was deployed participating in offsite job fairs, referral bonuses, and re-engagement of past applicants yet nothing moved the needle to the end goal.

That's where my innovation stepped in. If I couldn't find qualified talent, I would create it by building a supply pipeline of talent.

The organization had certified trainers in component identification and soldering. A partnership formed with a local career center to launch a free 40-hour training program. Anyone who completed the course and passed two certification exams would be eligible for employment. To make it accessible and enticing, breakfast, lunch, and a certificate of completion were provided.

More than 500 applications arrived at a single career fair. After applicant screening, 50 participants were invited. On day one, 40 showed up. By the end of the week, 20 remained. From that group, 10 employees were hired.

Given the labor market at the time, that return on investment was powerful. A testament to what becomes possible when fear stops driving limitation and starts fueling innovation.

Reflection Questions

- When was the last time fear showed up in your leadership journey?
- What assumptions or beliefs did it trigger?
- How might you use that insight to lead differently?

Manager Takeaway

Fear can distort your leadership lens, narrow your focus and pull you off course. Instead of letting fear drive your decisions, pause and reflect. Ask yourself what's underneath the urgency or self-doubt. Once named, fear loses its grip. And in that space, creativity, innovation, and confident leadership can flourish.

22

Managing Up: Turning Tough Bosses into Your Best Teachers

What Difficult Bosses Teach Us About Leading Ourselves

WHEN YOU'RE ASKED to lead, will you be ready to influence, have courage and the ability to navigate the power dynamics that exist?

Every difficult boss is a mirror, reflecting not just their flaws, but the parts of ourselves we're meant to strengthen. Throughout your career journey, you'll encounter every kind of boss imaginable. Some will inspire and challenge you to grow. Others will test your patience, confidence, and resilience. The truth is, you'll probably learn just as much—if not more—from the bad bosses as you do from the good ones.

No matter what kind of leader you work for, you can learn to manage up. Part of being an effective employee is helping your boss be successful. That doesn't mean being a "yes" person; it means being proactive in understanding what they need—and asking for what you need—to help them achieve success.

The reality is that no one at work is going to automatically get in line to champion you. You have to be your own advocate and activate your inner strengths to guide your path forward.

The Narcissist Boss: When Ego Runs the Show

Early in my retail career, I was training to become a store manager under a district manager named Carl, a textbook narcissist. Each time he came into my store, he found something to criticize. He didn't appreciate it when I asked clarifying questions or challenged his assumptions. Everything had to be his way.

Carl once told me flat out that I would *never* be a manager, that I didn't have what it took. I pressed for examples, but he couldn't give me one. That moment revealed more about his limitations than mine.

Belief in oneself is more powerful than any boss's opinion.

Instead of letting his words define me, I focused my energy on developing others and running my store with purpose. If Carl wasn't going to invest in me, I decided I would invest in myself.

Six months later, I was promoted to store manager. My first call was to Carl. I probably shouldn't have taken such delight in telling him how wrong he was, but I did. Over time, as I continued to advance and he eventually lost his position, it felt like poetic justice. Each new promotion was a quiet reminder that belief in oneself is more powerful than any boss's opinion.

Leadership Pause: Notice What You Notice

When you enter a room, a meeting, or a conversation, what do you see first?
Do you look for what's broken, or do you acknowledge what's working?
Great leaders know what they *choose* to notice, communicate what they *truly* value.
Before you speak, take a pause, collect your thoughts. See the effort, not just the flaws.

The Controlling Boss:
When Growth Becomes a Threat

There are some managers who try to block your growth; not because you lack ability, but because they're selfish. They can't imagine you moving on, because your departure would create more work for them. That was Abby's story.

Abby's career had soared quickly, earning her an executive title at a young age. But her rapid rise meant she skipped the learning that comes from experience. I had taken the long road, earning each step through hard lessons, persistence, and humility.

When Abby traveled (which she did often), I stepped up to lead. The team performed smoothly, sometimes even better than when she was there. Her peers began coming directly to me and Abby's ego couldn't handle the shift.

When I applied for a higher-level role outside of my department, she initially encouraged me until my offer came through. The position was suddenly downgraded to a lateral move. Abby had blocked my promotion. That moment revealed her true character, and I knew I could no longer work for someone who valued control over integrity.

When I resigned, she cried, telling me she was losing her "best friend at work." But leadership isn't about friendship, it's about empowerment. True leaders let others rise, even when it means they'll be outshined.

Leadership Pause: Letting Others Rise

Leadership isn't about holding others back, it's about propelling them to move forward, even when it stretches you. True leaders measure success not by how many people they manage to keep under their control, but by how many they've helped grow, mentor, and release to greater things.

Take a moment to reflect:

- Have you ever unintentionally limited someone else's growth because of fear or ego?
- Who on your team might be ready for their next step and how can you support them without hesitation?
- What does *real* success look like when you redefine it through the lens of shared growth?

When we have the courage to let others rise, we elevate the entire organization—and ourselves—with them.

Managing a Narcissistic Boss

If you've ever worked for someone like Abby or Carl, you know how exhausting it can be when everything revolves around their ego. Narcissistic leaders crave admiration but rarely offer it. The key to surviving, and even thriving, is to lower your expectations for validation and focus on what *you* can control.

See their behavior for what it is; not a reflection of your worth, but a mirror of their insecurity. Align your ideas with their self-interest, not to feed their ego, but to move the work forward. When you make them look competent, you create space to do your best work under the radar. Understand that they'll likely take credit when things go well and deflect responsibility for failures.

Abby had a reputation for collecting credit—often for work she didn't do—including mine. The company was in the thick of growing pains: duplicated efforts, wasted resources and systems breaking under pressure. Senior leadership asked for ideas from those closest to the work to drive efficiency and real change.

With a background in process improvement, I proposed creating a business improvement function, one that would report to my boss and be led by me. I built the framework, defined the scope, and mapped the impact. When I walked Abby through the plan, she was energized and I suggested we present it together at an upcoming mixed leadership meeting with both her senior-level peers and my director-level colleagues.

The meeting started; Abby took the floor and presented the plan as if it were hers, layering in her perspective but relying almost entirely on my work. In that moment, her insecurity was unmistakable. Visibility, not collaboration, was the priority.

I didn't interrupt her. I didn't correct her in the room. I chose strategy over satisfaction. Later, in private, I said, *"I'm glad you were able to use my plan in a way that supports your goal of improving efficiency."* It was a boundary disguised as professionalism and she heard it.

She took the credit, but she didn't take the substance. The room had already seen my thinking, my language, and my credibility. That experience reinforced a hard-earned truth: insecure leaders chase the spotlight. Confident ones leave fingerprints everywhere.

Safeguard yourself by scheduling formal checkpoints at 25%, 50%, and 75% completion milestones to secure their buy-in and document progress.

Insecure leaders chase the spotlight. Confident ones leave fingerprints everywhere.

Suggested structure:

- **25%:** Confirm your understanding of the task and clarify expectations for resources and deliverables.
- **50%:** Engage them for their input mid-project. Adjustments are easier to pivot midstream than to start over later.
- **75%:** Conduct a final review to validate alignment. Ask, "Do you see this leading to a successful outcome?" or "Are there any final barriers we should anticipate?" This fosters shared accountability and reduces future blame.

These checkpoints establish mutual ownership, reinforce your credibility, and limit unnecessary conflict and finger pointing later. Managing up in this context is not manipulation, it is strategic influence guided by emotional intelligence.

And remember, real leadership is not about ego, it's about growth. Even under a narcissistic boss, you can still lead with integrity, resilience, and quiet confidence.

The Bully Boss — Confronting Fear-Based Leadership

Have you ever worked for a boss who led through fear rather than inspiration? The kind who believed yelling louder or enforcing more rules equaled better performance? If so, you've seen firsthand how this approach destroys trust, engagement, and motivation.

If you've ever witnessed a command-and-control manager in action, you know it doesn't work, at least not in a modern business environment. Bob was one of those leaders. Coming from a military background, he believed barking orders and instilling fear would drive results. Maybe that worked in his past life, but in a manufacturing company filled with skilled, diverse, and hardworking employees, it failed miserably.

Ironically, Bob didn't even follow the rules he enforced. Before entering the production floor, all employees were required to wear grounding straps, carbon smocks, and special footwear to prevent electrical damage to components. Yet Bob—keys swinging, voice booming—was often the first to violate these safety measures while loudly reprimanding others for doing the same.

His management style was pure intimidation. Instead of learning his employees' names, he shouted orders over the intercom system, publicly summoning people to "call his extension immediately." When someone worked a full shift, he'd sarcastically ask if they were "working a half-day." His department was the largest in the organization, yet he never took the time to connect with the people doing the real work.

The factory floor was a vibrant mix of cultures; Puerto Rican, Jamaican, Vietnamese, Chinese, Korean, Polish, and Russian. And these employees took pride in what they did. Many personalized their workstations with family photos or stickers, small reminders of homes that made long shifts bearable. Bob couldn't stand it. He ordered all personal items removed, stripping the floor of warmth and connection. What was once an engaged workforce becoming disengaged and disheartened.

By month's end, when Bob needed "all hands-on deck" to meet production goals, he'd beg for overtime help. But motivation doesn't thrive under fear. The results, speak for themselves; targets were missed, morale sank, and trust evaporated. That's when Bob's director, Callie, stepped in to ensure the production goals were met. She did the opposite of Bob. She motivated through kindness, appreciation, and shared purpose. She brought in pizza, thanked everyone for their effort, and infused fun into the frenzy. When Bob tore people down, Callie built them back up month after month. It was inspiring, but exhausting.

The breaking point came one morning when an employee ran into my office, panicked, saying Bob was screaming profanities in a meeting upstairs. When I arrived, I could hear the yelling before the elevator doors even opened. I knocked, stepped in, and saw a room full of red faces and teary eyes. I calmly asked, "Is everyone okay in here?" Bob snapped that he was in a meeting and slammed the door.

A few hours later, he summoned me to his office. He was short and stocky, sitting on pillows behind a massive mahogany desk, trying to assert dominance. I, standing tall in heels, took a seat across from him. Within seconds, he began shouting. I stood, extended my hand, and said firmly, "When you can speak to me like an adult, not a two-year-old, we'll continue this conversation." Then I walked away. He followed, still yelling, but I didn't turn back.

Later, we were both called to the President's office. Bob expected me to back down. I didn't. The President reprimanded him, though no real consequences followed. But something shifted that day, Bob learned that his intimidation tactics didn't work on me. More importantly, the employees saw someone stand up to him.

I realized that silence only feeds toxicity. When bad behavior goes unchallenged, it grows roots. So I kept confronting it professionally, consistently, and without fear. It wasn't easy, but it was necessary. Those employees deserved a voice, and I chose to be that voice.

Lesson Learned:
You can't ignore bullies in leadership roles. Their power thrives on fear and compliance. The only way to dismantle it is to confront it with composure, courage, and conviction. Holding toxic leaders accountable, not only protects people; it restores the dignity of the workplace.

Leadership Pause: Stand Up, Speak Out

Think about a time when you witnessed or experienced intimidating behavior at work.

- How did you respond—or not respond—and why?

- What did it cost you or others to stay silent?
- What would courage look like for you in a similar moment today?

Leadership isn't about being fearless; it's about being brave enough to act, even when fear is present. Sometimes, the greatest form of leadership is simply refusing to look away.

The Spineless Boss: When Indecision Leads to Chaos

Then there's the boss who won't decide. They're overly cautious, and afraid. Afraid of being wrong, upsetting someone or owning the outcome. So instead of leading, they stall. Decisions drift and eventually, whoever speaks the loudest sets the direction rather than being based on logic or sound judgment.

At the time, I was running a program that was thriving in a brutally competitive market. Marketing dollars were scarce, but I identified a smart, cost-effective way to stand out and attract more people to the revenue pipeline. I put together a clear strategy, rationale, and return. My boss agreed it was creative and solid. Then came the familiar pattern: hesitation, deflection, and silence. He didn't want to make the ask or go to bat. So, nothing happened.

Weeks turned into months. Momentum stalled, not because the idea wasn't good, but because leadership lacked a spine.

I wasn't willing to let the program suffer and took initiative. I brought in outside partners to underwrite a breakfast program and materials needed for exposure. As a certified facilitator, I volunteered my time and redirected the limited budget toward assessments that strengthened the leadership development offering. The program was launched, succeeded and became a competitive differentiator.

Progress doesn't wait for courage, but it rewards those willing to act.

This is the reality of working for a spineless boss: waiting is the biggest risk. Managing up means stepping into the vacuum they leave behind. You make informed decisions, move the work forward, and accept that forgiveness may come easier than permission.

It's not reckless, it's necessary. When leadership hesitates, high performers don't sit idle. They drive the conversation, set the meetings, and force clarity where there is none. Sometimes, managing up means being the adult in the room. Progress doesn't wait for courage, but it rewards those willing to act.

The Meddler Boss: When Trust Is Missing

One of my clients, a capable CFO, worked for a president who couldn't stop interfering. Despite hiring strong leaders, he micromanaged every decision, from major financial strategies down to small survey approvals.

What could have been a trusting, empowered C-suite became paralyzed by constant second-guessing. Eventually, turnover at the top began to cascade through the organization, spreading dysfunction and frustration. Even well-intentioned "connection" efforts, like hosting monthly breakfast meetings with pre-approved questions, became symbolic of the organization's lack of authenticity.

If you find yourself working for a meddler, the best approach is to use data and missed-opportunity framing. I often use the phrase, *"help me to understand"* to put the ownership on me when I need to reframe a situation. The phrase pre-empts any potential defensive posturing or stance. Gently but clearly show how delays and over-control hurt results. If that doesn't work, you may eventually need to move on, because thriving under distrust is nearly impossible.

In this case, my clients' redundant tactics helped release the reins a bit with this leader, however it was not enough. The CFO continued to feel stifled and left the organization.

The Ghost Boss:
Never There When You Need Them

Frustration immediately comes to mind when I think about a previous boss I like to call *the Ghost.* There are plenty of problems I can solve on my own and decisions I'm confident making, but every so often, you reach that point where only your boss can make the call. And that's when you need them most… but they're nowhere to be found.

You check their calendar and it says "Available." You stop by their office, empty. They often say, *"I'm here for you, whatever you need…"* but that promise seems to vanish the moment you actually do.

I once coached an HR leader who also had a ghost boss. Without fail, if it was a sunny spring afternoon, he'd disappear, most likely squeezing in nine holes at the nearby golf course. Every critical decision stalled because he simply wasn't around.

So how do you get what you need from a Ghost Boss?

Start by anticipating the key decisions that require their input. Proactively schedule check-ins around times you know they'll be available, perhaps before or after meetings with their own boss. Build a cadence that works for both of you. I've even been known to camp outside my boss's office, catching them on their way to another meeting just to get a quick decision and keep things moving.

Another time, I learned my boss got soup from the same café every day at noon. I started timing my lunch order to match, riding the elevator back up together to get a two-minute weigh-in. Sometimes, you must be creative to get the guidance you need.

(One of my clients once confessed to following her boss into the men's room for a quick decision… now *that's* going too far!)

Ultimately, the key is to help your boss see that when they're unavailable, the work (and by extension, *their goals*) can't move forward. When they understand that their absence creates a bottleneck for both of you, it often inspires a bit more urgency and accessibility.

Leadership Pause:

When you encounter a Ghost Boss, don't waste energy resenting their absence; use it as a chance to sharpen your influence and adaptability. Think creatively about how to secure their attention and advocate for what you need to keep advancing your goals.

The Clueless Boss — Missing the Human Side of Leadership

Every leader leaves an imprint; not just through results, but through the way they make people feel. Emotional intelligence isn't about perfection; it's about awareness. This story is a reminder that when leaders fail to see the human side of performance, they unintentionally diminish motivation, trust, and engagement.

I was a young, inexperienced manager running a retail store in a busy mall. The previous manager had set a difficult example: working unreasonably long hours, rarely taking a day off, and trying to do everything alone. Ironically, despite all that effort, the store's results told a different story. The sales floor was a mess, cashiers weren't trained and ignored customers, and the backroom was so cluttered that you could barely make it to the office.

When I took over, my priority was to meet with each team member to understand whether they knew what was expected of them, what they wanted to learn, and how they liked to be appreciated. Once I identified the gaps, I began training and assigning responsibilities that didn't exist under the previous manager. It didn't take long before I noticed employees taking pride in their work and embracing the changes.

One of our first projects was transforming the sales floor. We cleaned, reorganized, and created an inviting, well-merchandised space. Within months, customers noticed. Sales climbed, and complaints dropped.

Next came the backroom, where chaos ruled. There were no systems, no order, just piles of merchandise wherever someone found space. Determined to fix it before my district manager, Mary, visited, I poured everything I had into the turnaround;

working 60–80 hours a week for two months. By the day of her visit, the store looked completely different. I was proud and eager to show her what we'd achieved.

When Mary arrived, she walked right past the cashiers without a greeting and headed straight to the office. She'd been in the store less than five minutes when she ran her finger across the two-way mirror and said, "Your windows are dirty. You'd better clean them today."

Something in me snapped. Exhausted and stunned, I grabbed the glass cleaner and paper towels, slammed them on the desk, and said, "You're clueless and clearly not paying attention to what matters!"

I explained everything the team had accomplished—the sales growth, training, and transformation—and how disappointed I was that none of it seemed to register.

A week later, Mary called me to lunch. She said my response was inappropriate and wrote me up for it. It was hard to take her seriously; she looked like a cartoon character in her pink polka-dot skirt, bow, and bright shoes… but the message stuck with me.

Looking back, I can see where I went wrong. My frustration boiled over, and I let emotion override professionalism. But I also learned a lasting leadership lesson: **pay attention to what truly matters.**

Mary missed a huge opportunity to acknowledge progress, celebrate her team's efforts, and reinforce the culture of pride we were building. Instead, she focused on fingerprints.

That experience shaped me. I learned how to manage up; documenting progress, creating paper trails, and not taking her lack of awareness personally. Most importantly, I learned that appreciation, connection, and recognition drive performance far more than criticism ever could.

Managing up in this situation requires translation because she could not understand what drove performance. I had to stop assuming she saw the store and the work in the way I did.

Consider this:

- Learn to speak the language your boss values most
- Connect through **metrics and data** when numbers drive their decisions
- Demonstrate how the work **improves perception or optics** when visibility matters to them
- Frame ideas around **efficiency, time savings, cost reduction, or risk mitigation** when operational impact is their priority

Leadership Pause: Turning Pain into Power

Every boss you encounter—good, bad, or somewhere in between—has something to teach you. The key is to shift from frustration to observation. Ask yourself:

- What is this situation teaching me about the kind of leader I *want* to become?
- What strengths am I developing as I learn to manage up, adapt, or push through?
- How can I use these lessons to lead with more integrity, empathy, and courage?

The Empowering Leader — Leading from Behind

Throughout this chapter, we've explored lessons from the difficult bosses, the ones who led through fear, ego, or control. But here's the hopeful truth: leadership is not fixed. It's fluid, learnable, and always evolving. Every ineffective habit can be unlearned, and every positive behavior can be cultivated. Emotional intelligence is the foundation of that growth, and its first cornerstone is self-awareness.

If you recognize traces of those challenging bosses in your own style, see that awareness not as a flaw, but as a gift. Self-awareness is your invitation to grow. Use the *Leadership Pauses* throughout this book to reflect, realign, and reset. The moment you recognize a blind spot, you've already taken the first step toward becoming a more authentic, intentional, and inspiring leader.

While stories of poor leadership abound, *great leaders* do exist and when you experience one, you never forget them.

These leaders are magnetic. They attract people wherever they go, often drawing team members from past roles because others trust and believe in them. They don't need the spotlight or the loudest voice in the room, they shine by helping others shine.

They communicate with clarity and transparency, not manipulation. They celebrate their teams publicly and coach privately. They assign stretch projects that challenge and grow their people, knowing that real development happens just beyond the comfort zone. They share credit freely, own their mistakes humbly, and transform failures into powerful lessons.

A great leader removes obstacles before anyone stumbles over them. They don't blame or deflect when things go wrong, they take responsibility, learn, and move forward strongly. Their teams feel seen, supported, and empowered. The proof shows up everywhere: higher engagement, stronger performance, and lasting loyalty. But their greatest achievement isn't results, it's *legacy*. They leave behind better leaders than themselves.

One leader who embodied all of these traits was named Grace. She was no-nonsense when it came to accountability, yet approachable and grounded. Grace had a rare gift for instantly disarming ego and stretching you beyond your comfort zone while simultaneously giving you the confidence to believe you could do it. She had a remarkable ability to see the big picture and understand exactly how each piece fit together, including how to bring out the best in every person.

When Grace was promoted to a larger role, her boss asked her to recommend a few potential successors. To my surprise, she submitted only one name: mine. I was stunned and deeply grateful. Grace had quietly prepared me for that moment. She believed in my potential, trusted me to lead my peers, and in doing so, changed the course of my career. That moment marked the true beginning of my journey in Human Resources.

I witnessed that same kind of empowering leadership years later while coaching on a ranch in Colorado, surrounded by wild horses, towering mountains, and the calming sound of a waterfall. It was the perfect setting to be reminded that *natural leadership is rooted in trust*.

We used the metaphor of dogsledding to describe it: when you've hired the right team, trained them well, and built a foundation of trust, you don't need to lead from the front. True leaders "mush from behind": guiding, supporting, and steering only when needed. The team knows the direction because they've been empowered to run their own course.

Leadership isn't about being out front, it's about knowing when to step aside so others can lead.

Leadership Pause: Mush from Behind

True leadership isn't about control, it is about cultivating trust so deep that your team can run confidently, even when you're not in sight.

- Who follows you and why?
- What legacy of leadership do you want to leave behind?
- How can you "mush from behind" by empowering others to lead while you guide, support, and celebrate their success?

True leadership isn't about control, it is about cultivating trust so deep that your team can run confidently, even when you're not in sight.

23

Threads to Thrive

Applying Lessons, Leading Yourself and Amplifying Impact

LEADERSHIP ISN'T A destination, it's a practice shaped by the moments that challenge you, the people who stretch you, and the choices that reveal who you truly are. Every story in this book has offered glimpses into that journey, from stepping forward before you feel ready to balance empathy with accountability and believing in yourself and others. Now, it's your turn: I have created the RIPPLE™ Coaching Framework that provides a simple, practical way to turn insight into action, helping you lead yourself and others with focus, courage, and lasting impact.

Now, the focus shifts.

Up to this point, you've been invited to reflect, to recognize patterns, and to see yourself more clearly. This chapter is about integration, how you take what you've learned and use it intentionally. Not just to lead others, but to lead yourself. Not just in big moments, but in the quiet, everyday decisions that shape your impact over time.

Where Change Actually Begins

Change rarely announces itself with a dramatic turning point. More often, it begins quietly, with a pause, a question, or the honest realization that something isn't working the way it once did. Growth doesn't require reinvention; it requires intention. When you slow down long enough to name what's really happening beneath the surface, you create space to choose differently.

Empowerment isn't about becoming someone new. It's about leading yourself with clarity, courage, and accountability, right where you are.

Introducing the RIPPLE™ Coaching Framework

The RIPPLE™ Coaching Framework was created to support this kind of intentional leadership. It brings together the themes and threads woven throughout this book into a simple, human-centered approach you can reuse. RIPPLE turns awareness into action, without feeling overwhelmed or letting perfectionism get in the way of small steps of progress.

Each step of the framework invites you to reflect honestly, take ownership, and practice differently. It helps you apply what you've already learned; whether you're navigating a difficult boss, setting boundaries, rebuilding confidence, or guiding someone else through change.

Like a rock hitting the water creating a ripple effect: small, deliberate changes create impact far beyond the moment they begin.

RIPPLE™ Coaching Framework

A simple, human-centered model for creating robust, meaningful and sustainable change

R — Reflect (insight begins with honest reflection)

Pause to notice what's really happening

- What's the current reality (facts, feelings, patterns)?
- What's being avoided, minimized, overworked or untested?
- What's the cost/risk of the status quo?

I — Identify

Name the core challenge or opportunity (clarity replaces feeling of overwhelm)

- What's the real issue beneath the surface?
- What belief, fear, or assumption drives this?
- What's within your control?

P — Prioritize

Choose what matters most right now (grounded in focus to fuel progress)

- Where will a shift make the biggest difference?
- What's one behavior, decision, or boundary to focus on?
- What are you saying yes and no too?

P — Plan

Design intentional, doable action (confidence grows through action)

- What specific action(s) will you take by when?

- What support, structure, or accountability is needed?
- How will you measure success?

L — Lead

Practice the shift consistently and visibly (modeling leadership)

- How will you show up differently? In words, tone, and behavior?
- How will you model this for others?
- What does self-leadership look like here?

E — Evaluate

Pause to reflect, learn and adjust (acceleration of growth)

- What worked? What didn't?
- What feedback are you hearing?
- What needs to be refined, reinforced or let go?

Coaching Yourself, Coaching Others

This framework is not reserved for formal coaching sessions. It's designed to help you coach yourself through moments of uncertainty and coach others through growth. The same questions that unlock clarity for a client can unlock clarity for you. The same pauses that build trust in a team can build trust with yourself.

RIPPLE is not a one-time exercise. It's a living practice that you can refer to whenever you feel stuck, stretched, or ready for more. In the pages that follow, you'll see how to use it to translate insight into action and intention into sustainable change.

The Heart of Coaching

Coaching is hard work, but it's some of the most meaningful work there is. Every person brings their own story, strengths, and barriers. My role as a coach has never been to give answers, but to ask questions that help others see what's possible beyond their current view.

Growth requires courage, commitment, and consistency. When someone leans in, momentum follows. When resistance shows up, the work becomes meeting it with empathy, honesty, and persistence.

Coaching is deeply personal. There is no single path, no universal solution. Sometimes growth comes from building new skills or strategies. Other times, it comes from quieting old stories of self-doubt and remembering what's already true. Coaching isn't about fixing what's broken; it's about amplifying what already exists.

Carrying the Lessons Forward

What follows are Coaching Nuggets and Leadership Lessons drawn from real experiences, moments that reveal both the art and heart of growth. My hope is that something in these stories resonates, offering a mirror, a guide, or a gentle nudge forward.

There is no finish line in leadership, only continued evolution. The most rewarding moments are when someone shares a win they once believed was impossible. Those moments are reminders that when we lead ourselves well, the ripple extends farther than we can see.

Let these lessons support you as you continue to grow; coaching yourself, leading others, and shaping impact that lasts.

RIPPLE™ Coaching Framework – A lesson in action:

Allie: Lead with Connection, Not Credentials

Allie was brilliant, so much so that she quickly rose into an executive leadership role. But her strength became her stumbling block. She led with *knowledge* instead of *connection*. When meeting new colleagues, she would start by listing her impressive credentials rather than taking time to get to know them.

Together, we shifted her focus from proving herself to growing others. By adopting a coaching mindset, Allie began using her expertise to *develop* and *support*, not to *impress*. The walls came down. Her team no longer saw her as distant; they saw her as authentic, approachable, and inspiring.

R — Reflect

Allie's reality was impressive on paper but strained in practice. She was highly accomplished, fast-tracked into an executive role, and deeply knowledgeable. Yet the emotional temperature in the room told a different story: distance, guarded conversations, and limited trust.

What was happening beneath the surface was subtle but costly. In her effort to establish credibility, Allie over-relied on credentials and under-invested in connection. She wasn't listening long enough to understand her people, and they, in turn, weren't fully leaning in.

Cost of the status quo:
Respect without trust. Authority without influence. A capable leader whose impact was capped by emotional distance.

I — Identify

The real issue wasn't competence; it was how competence was being used. Allie's belief that she needed to **prove** herself was driving her behavior. Credentials became armor rather than a bridge.

At the core was a quiet fear: *If I don't establish my expertise immediately, I won't be taken seriously.*

What was within her control wasn't how others perceived her résumé, it was how she showed up in a relationship. Influence didn't require more credentials; it required more curiosity.

P — Prioritize

The greatest leverage point wasn't changing strategy or structure; it was changing presence.

Allie chose one clear priority:
Lead conversations with curiosity instead of credentials.

That meant saying *no* to leading with titles, achievements, and authority, and saying *yes* to questions, listening, and shared ownership. The goal wasn't to impress, but to invest.

P — Plan

Allie committed to specific, visible shifts:

- Begin meetings by asking questions instead of sharing expertise
- Spend the first minutes of one-on-one conversations learning about the person, not the problem
- Use her knowledge to coach and develop, not to dominate discussions

She measured success not by how often she spoke, but by how often others did and how willing they were to engage honestly.

L — Lead

Over time, Allie showed up differently. Her tone softened. Her listening deepened. Her expertise didn't disappear, yet it became a tool for empowerment rather than a spotlight.

She modeled self-leadership by resisting the urge to prove and choosing instead to trust. In doing so, she gave her team permission to contribute, grow, and lead alongside her.

The shift was unmistakable: walls lowered, dialogue opened, and influence expanded.

E — Evaluate

The feedback told the story. Her team described her as approachable, supportive, and authentic. Engagement improved. Conversations became more candid. Trust replaced tension.

What worked was leading with connection first and credentials second. What needed reinforcement was consistency and continuing to choose relationships over recognition.

Coaching Nugget:
Your experience opens doors, but relationships keep them open. Lead with curiosity and connection before credentials. That's where real influence begins.

Lesson from Ben: Share the Vision So Others Can Build the Path

Ben was a strategist with a clear and compelling vision for his department's future. The challenge? The map for that future lived only in his head. While he could see the destination, his team couldn't, which left them uncertain about where to begin.

When Ben learned to articulate his vision and involve his team in shaping it, everything shifted. He began to have monthly combined leadership meetings to communicate his vision and thinking while using it as a chance to gather input. Additionally, he would send a bi-weekly email on progress to reinforce his message. Together, with his leadership team, they broke the big picture into milestones, celebrated small wins, and gained momentum towards shared goals.

Coaching Nugget:
A vision only becomes powerful when it's shared. Don't just hold the map, teach others how to read it. Leadership isn't about seeing the future alone; it's about bringing others with you.

Lesson from Callie: Balance Vision with Presence

Callie stepped in as her team's fourth leader in three years, a team weary of change and craving stability. She earned trust quickly by empowering others, encouraging collaboration, and giving people room to lead. For the first time in years, the team felt hopeful.

Callie's gift was vision: fast-thinking, strategic, always focused on the next big goal. But her team needed her presence here and now. They needed her to slow down, to translate her vision into practical, daily action.

When Callie learned to balance her forward focus with intentional presence, her leadership deepened. She didn't abandon her vision, she grounded it. The result was a team that not only believed in the future but knew how to build it.

Callie set up a series of retreats, professional development opportunities for each member of the team to use their strengths that grounded her in each of their areas.

Coaching Nugget:
A great leader keeps one eye on the horizon and one on the ground. Vision ignites the future, but presence fuels the progress.

Lesson from Doug: Pause Before You Push

Doug was known as the leader who got things done. Driven and decisive, he prided himself on speed and results. But his "fire, aim, ready" approach—moving fast and fixing faster—left a trail of burnout and frustration behind him.

In his rush to solve problems, Doug skipped an essential part of leadership: *thinking*. He often reacted before understanding, which created tension and eroded trust.

Through coaching, Doug discovered the power of the pause. Taking even a few moments to reflect before responding allowed him to see clearly, engage his team thoughtfully, and make better decisions. The results were immediate: stronger trust, smoother communication, and more sustainable performance.

He invited his peers to hold him accountable, giving them explicit permission to call him out when he slipped back into old habits. To slow his decision-making, he created a checklist of critical-thinking questions that forced him to pause before acting. Doug also sought out external peers to broaden his perspective and learn alternative approaches to decision-making.

Coaching Nugget:
Urgency gets things done, but reflection gets them done *right*. Slow down to speed up, your pause may be your most powerful leadership tool.

Lesson from Erin: Growing Into Your Greatness

Erin had spent nearly 15 years thriving in the medical field before making a bold career pivot into Human Resources. Within four years, she had risen from HR Assistant to HR Manager, earning growing responsibility and visibility.

But with visibility came vulnerability. A retired HR practitioner who chaired her Board questioned whether she was "strategic enough." His critique hit hard, triggering old insecurities: *I'm not good enough. I'm not ready. I don't want to fail.*

Through coaching, Erin realized she was already demonstrating strategic leadership, by aligning people priorities with organizational goals and building trust across the enterprise. The Board Chair's feedback reflected *his* need for relevance, not her lack of ability. Erin spent additional time with the Board chair giving him a broader perspective of her transferable skills and experience.

Once she owned her growth journey, Erin stopped striving to *prove* herself and started choosing to *lead*. She redefined what "strategic" meant in her role:

- It's not about knowing all the answers, it's about asking the right questions.

- It's about connecting today's actions to tomorrow's outcomes.
- It's about leading with confidence, even while still learning.

When Erin walked into her next Board meeting, she was grounded, prepared, and confident. Afterwards, she emailed: *"I crushed the meeting."* The Board Chair told her, "Erin, you've arrived as a respected HR professional." That sentence marked a turning point in her belief in herself.

Coaching Nugget:

- Growth requires grace. Discomfort means you're expanding.
- Confidence doesn't come from mastery; it comes from trust in your own learning process.
- Others may test your competence; don't let them define your capability.
- Strategic leadership begins when you stop proving and start leading.

Lesson from Faith:
Leading with Empathy and Accountability

Faith was a confident senior executive and a natural relationship builder. When she took over a regional business unit, she inherited a team loyal to her predecessor, a long-tenured leader who had selectively enforced expectations, creating a culture of blame and avoidance.

Faith knew she needed to reset accountability, but her empathetic style sometimes softened her message. Her feedback, though caring, was often received as optional rather than essential.

Through coaching, Faith learned that empathy and account-ability are not opposites, they're partners. When leaders communicate with both clarity and care, teams feel supported *and* responsible. Faith began delivering feedback that was direct, specific, and rooted in respect. She continued to impart expectations with consequences. When the deadline came and went, she followed up and followed through on what had been discussed. Over time, she drove real change without losing her warmth or authenticity.

Coaching Nugget:

- Empathy doesn't mean avoiding discomfort; it means caring enough to be clear.
- Accountability is an act of respect; it shows belief in others' potential.
- Authentic leadership blends care, candor, and consistency.

Reflection Questions:

1. Do you soften feedback to avoid conflict? What message does that send?
2. How can you balance care and candor in your next conversation?
3. What might accountability look like as an expression of belief in your team?

Lesson from Gary: Leading After a Legend

Gary stepped into one of the toughest leadership transitions imaginable, taking over a nonprofit from its beloved founder. The founder wasn't just well-respected; she was the heart of the organization. To make matters more complicated, her brother also worked there and was treated differently than the rest of the staff. He operated without boundaries, accountability, or structure.

In an effort to ensure a smooth handoff, the founder stayed on during Gary's first few months. But instead of supporting his leadership, her continued presence created confusion. Staff continued going to her for answers, approval, and direction, leaving Gary on the sidelines of his own role. Though unintentional, the founder's involvement undermined his credibility and delayed his ability to lead effectively.

Gary faced a difficult decision: maintain the comfort of keeping her around or claim his leadership identity and authority. With courage and respect, he chose the latter. He had an open, heartfelt conversation with her about how her presence, though well-meaning, was holding him back. Because she cared deeply about the mission and Gary's success, she understood. Together, they created a 90-day transition plan that allowed her to gracefully step away and gave Gary the autonomy he needed to lead.

Once that transition was complete, Gary faced another challenge... the founder's brother. As a former peer, the brother didn't respect Gary's authority and resisted change. He arrived late, ignored structure, and pushed forward ideas that weren't aligned with the organization's mission. Gary tried everything; coaching, setting expectations, even creating a performance improvement plan with clear accountability. But while the brother had the skills, he lacked the will to change.

Eventually, Gary made the tough but necessary call to terminate his employment. It wasn't about punishment, it was about protecting the organization's culture and the integrity of leadership. Gary learned that no matter how much you care or how hard you try, you cannot want success more than someone else wants it for themselves.

Gary's lesson is that leadership is not just about managing people, it's about owning your authority with compassion and conviction. You can honor what came before you, but you must also have the courage to lead forward.

Coaching Nugget:

- Transitioning after a beloved leader requires both humility and firmness. You honor the past while shaping the future.
- Boundaries build credibility. Without them, even the most well-intentioned transitions can blur authority.
- Skill without will is a leadership red flag. You can coach ability, but you cannot coach desire.
- Accountability protects culture. Sometimes the hardest decisions are the most necessary to uphold integrity and trust.
- Don't take resistance personally. When others refuse to grow, it reflects their choices—not your leadership.

Reflection Questions

1. When have you stepped into a role where someone else's influence still lingered? How did it impact your ability to lead?
2. What conversations do you need to have to clarify boundaries and strengthen your credibility?
3. How do you distinguish between someone who *can't* perform versus someone who *won't*?

Lesson from Hannah: Letting Go to Grow

Hannah grew up in her family's business, which was later acquired by a larger manufacturing company. She had done it all; rotating through departments, mastering the operations, and leading from the ground up. Without a college degree, she earned her credibility through experience and sheer determination.

But as the company grew, Hannah's perfectionism became her biggest limitation. Her "I'll just do it myself" approach left her buried in the details and overwhelmed by work. She dreamed of becoming a director, but her perfectionist grip on control kept her from leading strategically.

Together, we examined where her time and energy were going. She realized she was enabling her team's dependence by doing their work for them and holding impossibly high standards that even she couldn't meet.

By recalibrating expectations and embracing *progress over perfection*, Hannah learned to delegate effectively, empower others, and lead with trust. She also pursued a professional certification to strengthen her confidence and credibility. Six months later, she was promoted to Director, a testament to both her growth and her grit.

Coaching Nugget:

- Perfectionism often masks fear of failure, of judgment, or of not being enough.
- Delegation isn't losing control, it's multiplying impact.
- Credibility is built through confidence, consistency, and continuous learning.

Reflection Questions:

1. Where are you holding on to work that no longer belongs to you?
2. How might perfectionism be limiting your leadership potential?
3. What story about your background needs to be rewritten to reflect who you are *now*?

The Coaching Multiplier

Growth doesn't happen in isolation, it creates ripples. One shift in awareness, one courageous conversation, one moment of clarity and everything around you begins to move.

Faith found her strength in balance, learning that accountability and empathy can coexist. When she stood in that truth, her team began to rise with her. Communication opened, trust rebuilt, and ownership returned. Her clarity became contagious.

Hannah's story was one of courage, letting go of perfection to embrace possibility. When she released control, her confidence expanded. And when she stepped into her worth, others saw her differently too. Her transformation changed not only her career but also the culture around her.

That's what coaching does, it awakens what's already inside you. It reminds you that you were never meant to play small, that every step toward your best self leaves a trail for others to follow. When one person grows, others feel it. When one leader believes again, an entire team begins to believe too.

This is the ripple effect of coaching; where one conversation can change a life, a team, or even an organization.

24

Coaching from the Inside Out

Designing the Leader Your Becoming

WHEN YOU THINK about yourself a year ago, have you changed at all? It is likely you will answer a resounding yes! The world around you has shifted, and leadership has shifted with it. We're navigating accelerated change, constant volatility, and increasing complexity. Work no longer comes with clear edges or simple answers. And because of that, what it means to lead has fundamentally evolved.

If you feel uncertain about your next step, consider this your invitation to pause. Growth doesn't always mean climbing higher or faster. Sometimes the most meaningful progress comes from moving sideways, deepening your skills, or choosing a path that stretches you in a new way.

That reality is what inspired this book.

Leadership coaching matters now more than ever, not as a luxury or privilege, but as a practical way to grow, adapt, and stay grounded. **Coaching shouldn't be reserved for the few;**

it should be accessible to anyone willing to reflect, learn, and lead with intention.

You don't need permission, a title, or even a coach to begin. Self-coaching is the first leadership practice, and the one you'll return to most often.

You already carry stories of resilience, grit, and growth. Those lived experiences are your greatest teachers. When you reflect on them honestly, you begin leading yourself with clarity and confidence.

Momentum isn't built through big leaps. It's built through small, intentional steps. Choose one place to begin:

- Journal through a chapter using the RIPPLE lens
- Ask for feedback from a trusted colleague or friend
- Protect time on your calendar to reflect instead of reacting

As your journey unfolds, you may find that additional support accelerates your growth. Mentorship is one powerful option, and it doesn't have to come from your direct manager. Mentors can be found through professional associations, volunteer boards, alumni networks, peers, or even friends who challenge your thinking.

You may also choose to work with a leadership or executive coach. Coaching isn't about fixing what's broken. It's about strengthening what's already there. Even high performers need support as leadership demands new muscles, navigating difficult conversations, motivating diverse teams, and staying grounded through change.

Every coach brings a different approach. As a Gallup® Certified Strengths Coach, I focus on helping leaders leverage their natural talents. In using the CliftonStrengths® framework countless times it consistently shows that growth doesn't come from obsessing over weaknesses, but from using strengths intentionally to close gaps and expand capacity.

Coaching is practice. You will stumble. You will get uncomfortable. You will make mistakes. That isn't failure, it's transformation in motion.

Coaching is not corrective. It's a partnership for growth. And growth doesn't demand perfection; it asks for presence, curiosity, and willingness. Speaking as a recovering perfectionist, I can tell you, coaching changes how you lead, how you see yourself, and how you show up for others.

You can never go wrong investing in yourself.

At the beginning of this book, I invited you to take bold risks, pursue work that genuinely excites you, and consider stretch opportunities that expand your capabilities. That invitation still stands.

Your career isn't a ladder, it's a mosaic. Every role, project, and challenge adds a tile to the picture of who you're becoming.

If there's one truth I've learned, it's this:
You can never go wrong investing in yourself.

As you close this book, pause. Reflect. And begin designing your next chapter with intention.

Now that you have read the book, take action! Additional coaching reflections, activities, and leadership prompts not included in the book can be accessed here:
https://www.unapologeticonpurpose.com

Leadership Pause:
Crafting Your Career Action Plan

1. Reflect on Your Journey:

- What patterns, strengths, or lessons have surfaced across your career so far?
- Which personal chapters resonated with you the most?
- Which roles or experiences brought out your best self and why?

____

____

____

____

2. Redefine Success:

- Does your current definition of success still fit who you are today?
- What does success look like beyond a title or promotion? Will this fulfill you?

____

____

____

____

3. Identify Your Growth Edge:

- Where do you feel "stuck" or ready for something more?
- What skill, mindset, or behavior could you strengthen through coaching or mentoring?

____

____

____

____

4. Create Your Development Mosaic:

- List the transferable skills you've gained from each career chapter.
- Circle the ones that excite you most, those are the clues to your next opportunity.

____

____

____

____

5. Commit to Continuous Growth:

- Set one concrete development goal for the next six months.
- How will you measure your progress in small steps?

Seek a mentor, coach, or peer who can act as an accountability.

____

____

____

____

Review Inquiry

Hey, it's Kim here.

I hope you've enjoyed the book, finding it both useful and fun. I have a favor to ask you.

Would you consider giving it a rating wherever you bought the book? Online book stores are more likely to promote a book when they feel good about its content, and reader reviews are a great barometer for a book's quality.

So please go to the website of wherever you bought the book, search for my name and the book title, and leave a review. If able, perhaps consider adding a picture of you holding the book. That increases the likelihood your review will be accepted!

Many thanks in advance,

Kim Kenney-Rockwal

Will You Share the Love?

Get this book for a friend, associate, or family member!

If you have found this book valuable and know others who would find it useful, consider buying them a copy as a gift. Special bulk discounts are available if you would like your whole team or organization to benefit from reading this.

Just contact Kim@kimkenneyrockwal.com or
https://www.kimkenneyrockwal.com/.

Would You Like
Kim Kenney-Rockwal to
Speak to Your Organization?

Book Kim Now!

Kim Kenney-Rockwal accepts a limited number of speaking/coaching/ training engagements each year. To learn how you can bring her message to your organization, email kim@kimkenneyrockwal.com or visit https://www.kimkenneyrockwal.com/.

About the Author

 Kim Kenney-Rockwal, MBA, SPHR, is an executive coach and leadership development expert who partners with leaders to deepen self-awareness, expand emotional intelligence, and create sustainable growth from the inside out, grounded in strengths, not limitations. With more than 30 years of experience in human resources across four industries, Kim blends strategic insight with compassionate challenge to help leaders clarify their identity, align their actions, and lead with confidence and authenticity.

A dynamic keynote speaker and workshop facilitator, Kim brings her message to life through bold insights, powerful storytelling, and highly engaging experiences. She inspires audiences to disrupt limiting beliefs, activate their potential, and translate learning into immediate action. Kim is a certified Gallup® Strengths Coach and Master Practitioner in MBTI® and EQ-i 2.0® / EQ-i 360®, and the owner of KKR Coaching LLC. She lives in New England.

Kim Kenney-Rockwal can be reached at:
https://www.kimkenneyrockwal.com/
or email: Kim@kimkenneyrockwal.com.